WORDS OF PRAISE

*"**Life Upside Down*** is a book of deep intimacy, revealing the ways rough initiations can break us open to levels of transparency and vulnerability we rarely encounter. Throughout the story, Erlander invites us into the heart of love, with its fierce and exacting demand for our ripening, often stretching us beyond what we thought was possible. We are reminded, again and again, that the soul will use whatever befalls us and transform it into medicine. This book is healing itself. A deep bow of gratitude."

~Francis Weller, author of
***The Wild Edge of Sorrow:
Rituals of Renewal and the Sacred Work of Grief***

*"**Life Upside Down*** is an inspiring and deeply engaging story of grief, trauma, healing, rebirth, transformation, and ultimately love. Through her beautifully written, honest, and sometimes unapologetically raw account, we are captivated by the woven threads of this intricate story. Her courage, strength, and determination are apparent as we move with her through the myriad hurdles along this arduous path through the land of quadriplegia. Beth has written an engaging book that is a true testament to the human spirit, a journey of the soul that is imbued with wisdom encouraging others to keep moving forward regardless of what life has thrown at them."

~Cara Hope Clark
Award-winning author of ***Widow's Moon;
The Transformational Nature of Grief.***

"Beth's raw, intimate, and honest approach to sharing her journey is profoundly needed in our Western world which minimizes grief. It is in service to all who have stumbled through the shockwaves of an unimaginable loss. Grief is never meant to be held alone. This book will become an invaluable companion to anyone who has been launched into the role of caring for a loved one with a spinal cord injury. Moreover, this book is for all of us. Beth takes us with her through this labyrinth of life—you too are invited to walk this path of heartbreak and to awaken your deepest longing for life itself."

~Dr. Arielle Schwartz,
author of **The Post-Traumatic Growth Guidebook**
among her books on trauma recovery.

"Beth Erlander's book, **Life Upside Down, The Fall that Transformed Our Lives, Lifting Me Through Grief, Love and Quadriplegia**, is a stunning and brilliant exploration of life, love, loss, and growth. She takes us on a journey that is honest and educational. You will learn things you never thought to even ask about. You will gain an understanding of what it means to live, love, and grow while navigating a life-changing event as your partner becomes a quadriplegic. You will develop a deep compassion for Michael, her partner, and also, obtain an awareness that you didn't even know you needed. Beth's matter-of-fact way of navigating her journey (and Michael's) is beautiful. There are too many things in life that we don't talk about and address with honesty and openness. Beth invites you in, telling all the nitty-gritty and icky truths. It is truly stunning. I highly recommend that everyone read this book."

~Jessica Goldmuntz Stokes, Author of
**Seeking Clarity in the Labyrinth,
a Daughter's Journey Through Alzheimer's.**

"In **Life Upside Down**, Beth paints a canvas of human fragility and the intricate dance between love and sorrow. As Michael's life takes an unexpected turn, we're led through the woods of memory, intuition, and raw emotion—each step echoing with the mysteries of Lyons, Colorado. Like the art I make from nature's ephemeral beauty, this story captures the fleeting moments of pain, love, and the resilience it takes to rebuild from ruins. Let Beth's words guide you through a labyrinth of the human spirit, reminding us of the ever-present dance between despair and hope, shadows and light."

~Day Schildkret, Author of
Morning Altars and **Hello, Goodbye**

"If everyone could tell their story, how would our lives be different? I stepped away numerous times because of the intensity of Beth's raw, harrowing and honest memoir of her journey to love life even after her partner's bicycle accident turned it upside down. I needed to process what was so vividly described as utter despair, desperation, grief, longing, heartache, loss and lostness. Sticking with it, I am reminded by Beth's journey that our capacity, unknown to most of us, to hold, contain and grow is more than what we've ever imagined. She reveals how a crack in the heart lets more light in and I see that it also lets in more capacity to hold what life hands us. Beth's authentic way grows her into being human. As I listen to the tragedy and the love, I experience that pain and sorrow, grief and loss not only causes a crack that makes one become more of a human being, it transforms one into human loving. Love is our greatest teacher. Beth gives us a story of resistance and resilience, grief and opening to love; what is rend asunder can be rebuilt out of the ruins and remains of a life turned upside down.

This story is for everyone to read and pause and read and find that capacity to open more because shit happens. Beth walks hundreds of miles to earn her healing of what seemed insufferable and she learned, grew and now has filled that heart of hers because finding her way through this showed her that 'nothing else matters' but love. She and Michael are a thriving couple who have been called to live an unexpected life and to always listen deeply and act on this call to service."

~Deanna Jenné,
Traditional Healer

Life Upside Down

"Beautiful writing that captures the mind-body connection of instinct when the tragedy isn't apparent. There is no way to explain grief or what it does. But it doesn't stop the journey. Grief digs the journey out while gripping the life slipping from clutched fingers, a life that Beth was forced to let go."

~Cedar Sarilo
Author, Caregiver, Shamanic practitioner

"A true-life romance that reads like a thriller, Beth Erlander opens her heart in the midst of catastrophic life changes. Her beloved partner Michael has a near fatal accident, and Beth recounts the tale with the felt sense of a wizard. Her writing brings one into the moment, and she weaves together the time and space of a complex real life story, magically brought into heartfelt focus. The power of grief, of love, of dedication, and the personal journey to accept what life brings, is the gift of this book. For anyone who has had life changing circumstances, survived shock or trauma, or simply dealt with disappointment and change, *Life Upside Down* will rivet you to awareness. You will be asked to feel, grieve, contemplate, and engage those deeper questions of life that dance through the known and unknown. Might I say, "a must read," for anyone contemplating grief and resilience."

~Annie Brook, Ph.D, LPC, RSME (ISMETA)
Author, **Birth's Hidden Legacy**

LIFE

UPSIDE DOWN

The Fall That Transformed Our Lives,
Lifting Me Through Grief, Love and Quadriplegia

LIFE
UPSIDE DOWN

The Fall That Transformed Our Lives,
Lifting Me Through Grief, Love and Quadriplegia

Beth Erlander

Please note: All of the words in this memoir are my own, no AI was used.

Beth Erlander beth@betherlander.com

ISBNs:
Paperback: 979-8-9879323-0-8
eBook: 979-8-9879323-1-5

Publisher: Crow Flow Publishing, www.crowflowpublishing.com

Editor and Publishing Consultant: CSusanNunn@gmail.com
Cover Design: Pro_eBookcovers@Fiverr.com
Book Interior and E-book Design by Amit Dey | amitdey2528@gmail.com
Crow Flow logo and feather design: Brandi Price | https://www.brandipprice.com/

DEDICATION

To Michael,
for your love and perseverance and for never giving up on me.
To the rock that started it all,
thank you for holding our story in the bones of the earth.
And for all those in the upside-down world of grief,
may you find your medicine and rise to meet the morning light.

FOREWORD

Transformation
mid-14c., "change the form of" (transitive), from Old French
transformer (14c.), from Latin transformare "change in shape,
metamorphose," from trans "across, beyond"
(see trans-) + formare "to form"

This is a story of radical transformation. However, "transformation" does not convey or touch the depth of Beth's life-altering journey as she so candidly and with utter rawness shares in this book. Beth's story is one of descending into the darkest ruins of grief as a result of a searing and gutting life tragedy and through this "dark night of the soul" as coined by St. John of the Cross, eventually surrendering to and thoroughly allowing Grief to become her greatest teacher. Through being fiercely committed to her process, Beth harvested the light, wisdom, and power that grief can offer, and has applied it to living her most congruent life path.

On August 27, 2012, Beth and her partner Michael's lives as they knew them were decimated to the ground on which Michael fell as a result of a tragic mountain biking accident that left him quadriplegic.

Although their lives became completely unstitched, their love story as you will see, is what not only remained but continued to evolve into one of the strongest testaments of soul love.

Turned completely upside-down with no orientation or map, Beth's story brings us through the uncensored and searingly painful process of her grief journey as she navigates the world of quadriplegia with Michael and the extreme alterations of her life and self. Peppered with her irreverent, innate humor, Beth unapologetically shares and teaches the reader of many of these sobering realities. In this book, she normalizes grief in a culture that sanitizes and pathologizes it. She shows the reader the alchemical, life-affirming power and even joy that is possible in grief through complete surrender to what is. As a result of August 27th, 2012, Beth has contributed significantly to the importance of and normalization of grief expression and its capacity for transformation as she has grown into an expert grief therapist and ritualist.

It is a significant honor to write the forward for Beth's book. Through the unbelievable challenges of adjusting to a new, most heartbreaking, and stressful life that Beth has devotedly walked with Michael and her grief process, I have been gifted to witness her develop a fierce, soulful, and unabashed voice and embodied presence. Beth and I refer to each other as "Grief Warriors;" for knowing personally and professionally the sacredness of the terrain of surrendering everything to grief as a response to our personal tragedies. Dearest friends for decades, as well as psychotherapist colleagues and ritualists, I have watched Beth grow into and embody the wise words of holocaust survivor Viktor Frankl…"What is to give light must endure burning." Beth's light, even amidst the many ongoing hardships of her life shines like the Colorado sun where we live. My favorite person with whom to grieve, whether in ritual or in one of our homes where we wail, sob, spit, scream, writhe, and end up laughing so hard that our bellies ache, Beth is emblematic as an example of what is possible when one surrenders to the Muse of grief. To watch Beth's evolution personally and professionally has me bow with deep reverence to her and the ways in which she has been able to, even amidst life's unwanted tragedies, harvest the gems to share with the world.

~Merryl E. Rothaus, LPC, LMHC, ATR-BC, CHT, ACS
Boulder, Colorado
August 7th, 2022
www.merrylrothaus.com

ACKNOWLEDGMENTS

Giving birth to this story and getting it out to the world has been an act of love and devotion with moments of hard grit and push for sure! The seed was planted in the early days post-accident in the midst of the 'trauma drama' when I wrote late at night to update everyone on the Lotsa Helping Hands website. Writing settled me and kept me going. Thank you to all who were there in the beginning and read every one of my posts and held Michael and me close.

I would specifically like to thank those of you who helped me get this book written, published, and out to the wider world.

Thanks to Lisa Jones, my first official writing teacher. And thanks to the ones who attended the class in her dining room. Sitting at that table and seeing your teary eyes after I was done reading my pieces, is forever in my mind and heart.

Thanks to Tanja Pajevic, my second official writing teacher. I am deeply grateful for your nine-month memoir course. Your feedback and words of encouragement helped me continue to write my story and guide me to get this story published! Thanks to the ones who took that course with me and helped me mold this book from its beginning to where it is now.

Thanks to Susan Nunn, my editor, and publisher who in the process of birthing this book has become a dear friend. Thank you for your knowledge, wisdom, and calming words as I dealt with this stressful process of writing and publishing my very first book.

Thanks to my dearest peeps—the ones who have stayed with me and us from the beginning of this whole ordeal and continue to show up for us today. Thank you Linda Flinkman for being there whenever I needed you, for being my unofficial book launch manager, and for your words of encouragement. Thank you Michael Hahn and Elizabeth Rainey for the needed retreats and phone calls of love and encouragement. Thank you Tauna for always making me laugh and calling me back to the waters to play with you. Your post-it note that says—"I love you Betina! Your memoir is so needed in the world," is still straight ahead of me on my desk. And the other one telling me to "shake my ass" was also super helpful. Thanks, Merryl Rothaus for your Grief Warrior sisterhood and for saying yes to writing the beautiful forward for this book that made me cry with tears full of love and gratitude.

Many thanks to all my readers—Francis, Cedar, Day, Jessica, Cara Hope, Arielle, Annie, and Deanna. Thanks for taking the time out of your busy lives to drop into this story and come back with honest feedback and words of praise.

I'd like to thank myself for getting up early before the caregivers arrived to write in the early morning hours. Thanks for your dedication and for giving up precious hours of sleep to continue writing. (I am not a morning person!) I'd also like to thank my badass higher self for showing up and encouraging me to write my story and to share it with others and that it would indeed be handy one day.

Thank you to Francine Shapiro for creating EMDR. In the beginning, I wrote with headphones on when it was too hard to write about the trauma. The bilateral beeps kept me from being overwhelmed.

Thank you, Mark Johnson and Joel Bradst. You came and took care of Michael while I went away to the Camino or go on writing retreats. Thanks for your many years of devoted friendship with Michael.

Thanks to the trail in the foothills near our home in North Boulder. Thanks to the nature spirits that dwell there who gave me words and ideas on my walks. You also filled my heart with beauty and peace. Thank you to the other than human guides and companions–thank you to the tree near us for sending me visions of the book at the end of your branches. Thank you to the winged ones for your constant reminder to widen my vision. Thank you deer for your gentleness. Thank you Crow for calling Michael and me to work together. Thank you to my kitty Slinky for your hours of play on my writing breaks.

A deep heartfelt thanks to all my ancestors–you have had my back throughout this entire journey since the accident and the writing process. Thank you for your presence, support, and love. I am proud to be your granddaughter and great-granddaughter, etc. Thank you for being with me every step of the way. I feel you now more than ever and am so grateful for all of you. Your hardship and your perseverance to survive are what propelled me forward.

Thank you Didier Somé, Elder Malidoma's youngest brother, and thank you to the Kontomble. You all blessed the first early draft of my manuscript with your words and energy. Thank you for holding me and my book from the rich land of Africa.

Thank you to our caregivers for allowing me to have the time and space to work on this book. I couldn't have done it without you. And thanks to the ones who are still in touch with us today and are finally reading this beautiful love story.

Thank you Michael for being here throughout the entire process. For living it with me and then reliving it with me. Thanks for your willingness for me to tell our most vulnerable parts of the story. Thanks for encouraging me to be wickedly honest. Thanks for dealing with my lack of time while this book was being birthed. Thank you for being you…I love you.

And finally, I thank you, dear reader. Thank you for finding this book and giving your time and energy to read it. And if you are in the process of coming right side up, may my story be a beacon of hope for you.

TABLE OF CONTENTS

CHAPTER 1

THE ACCIDENT

"When we are no longer able to change a situation,
we are challenged to change ourselves."

—Victor Frankl

T hrough the oxygen mask in the ER, Michael said to me in a rapidly
trembling voice, "I'm really fucked up."

In my state of shock and numbness and feeling as if this were all a
bad dream, I said, "Yes, yes you are," as I scanned his body and nodded
my head up and down like a robot. He was shirtless and I was staring
at the dry red dirt on his manly hairy, leanly sculpted chest and biceps.

We were surrounded in the ER by the overly sanitized smooth
linoleum, stainless steel trays, plastic tubing, monitors, beepers, and
hospital staff, all moving really fast. The cold hard steel of the stretcher
he was laying on, body so still, yet shaking like small earthquakes. His
body was freaking out, trying to shake off the trauma of dura and bones
breaking; gritty crackling of things going very wrong inside. Bone texture
exploding, what does that sound like? Michael knows.

Just hours before, he had taken his last bike ride on his favorite trail near the town of Lyons, Colorado, called Hall Ranch. I now refer to it as Hell Ranch. He didn't know it was to be his last bike ride. He was on his way down and a fat drop of rain fell on him reminding him to do ceremony. He stopped and did a bit regarding clarity in his life and lineage...and he lost track of time. He noticed it was getting dark and realized he should get back on his bike and head down. He remembers thinking – I can't see that well; I should probably get off the bike and walk. But he didn't. Instead, he didn't see that five-inch protrusion of rock he hit. His front tire stopped immediately, and he instinctively squeezed the brakes while he and the bike flew up and over as one unit. His head hit the rock and then the bike fell on top of him. Thankfully he had his bike helmet on, however, because of how he landed, his neck hyper-flexed forward beyond what was normal, and then he heard that awful cracking sound.

Laying on the trail not being able to move, nor able to feel the pebbles underneath his flesh, poking into places and creating discomfort. Wanting to move but couldn't. Him, dusk light, it was beautiful, one of those late summer evenings in Colorado where you can feel the warm air on your skin. He panicked, yet he was thinking he would simply shake this off and get up and walk away and finish his ride.

But that moment didn't happen. He couldn't move. All he could move was his neck. He shook his neck from side to side too much. He wondered later if that actually did more damage to it. In a state of shock, and knowing I was the only one who knew where he was, he gathered all his energy and screamed my name.

I was at home cooking him a surprise dinner when suddenly I heard a call in my heart. It was an odd call, intuition, a sense of sadness that struck me deeply. I had to sit down on my dirty old plastic stool in the pure white tiled kitchen. Our small kitchen was just right in that moment holding me as I said out loud to myself, "God, I feel so sad." Then I asked myself why I felt such immense sadness…was it the fact we had been arguing a few days earlier? I continued cooking knowing I needed to apologize for my actions when he returned. Tuned in on some level, my body and heart knew what was happening, but I did not.

It was 8:09 p.m. when that odd intuitive call came through my senses. I was cooking roasted sweet potatoes and chicken while he was falling, cracking, breaking neck bones, and waiting, waiting. I too was waiting, waiting for him. By now he was really late and I started to worry. I listened to every single small noise around me, my ears gone hyper-vigilant; like a gentle deer's ears perking up and rotating to the incoming sound. I was attuned to cars pulling up in the townhouse parking lots, others' footsteps up those old stairs full of slivers that needed a serious redo, garages and neighbor's doors opening and closing, cars in the distance parking, turning, driving, voices coming and going. Life going on as usual while ours was in this odd liminal eerie pause. The crickets kept singing…

How I was hoping to hear him coming around the corner and up our small porch, talking passionately and loudly to either some new client explaining how the body works from the inside or to one of his sisters. This was a habit he did often – arriving home after being gone for a few days as he worked and lived part-time in Fort Collins. It used to make me angry, and at this moment, I was longing for him to show up in this way. How I wanted to hear him multitasking, talking on the phone while setting down all his bags of winter squash and dirty sheets from his workweek. Michael was an amazing osteopathic bodyworker who devoted many hours to helping his clients feel better in their bodies. Ironic, as he now lay on the ground waiting to be rescued.

While my sense of hearing was becoming more and more tuned to his arrival, up on the trail, I'm wondering now if Michael's sense of smell was working overtime. Could he smell the pine needles surrounding him? Were the trees alarmed and concerned, did they want to reach out and hold him if they could? Did he smell the red dirt trail as his head was so close to it? Did he smell the sage and the fresh air around him? What happens to your sense of smell when you are in a state of shock and panic? Are your senses attuned like a superpower or do they go dormant to save your energy? His nervous system was in overload for sure.

Did he hear the animals wandering and wondering about him? Were there any creatures that witnessed the accident – coyote, red tail hawk, owl? He was the last human on the trail, only his car left in the usually packed parking lot. Did he hear birdsong along with his neck breaking – the dura busting apart and C5 shattering? Did the crickets pause as they took in the scene – Michael on his bike carefully going down the trail, if he had moved just slightly, missing the one five-inch rock he would have been down to the bottom in about a minute or two. Our life could have carried on as usual and he would have arrived to have the dinner I was cooking for him.

The dinner I made – roasted chicken thighs with the skin crispy the way he liked it. It reminded him of "gripshas" – the fatty bits of chicken skin fried in oil by his grandma that he ate with her freshly baked bread. It simply melted in his mouth, and he would want to slow down time to fully take in the full flavor of fat and salt and crispy swirling around in his palate. Remember Maude's smell machine from the movie *Harold and Maude*? It is kind of like that but with tastes, he would want to break down each flavor to savor it all.

I didn't really take in the flavors of that meal, eating alone, and waiting and wondering – where the fuck was my partner? I sat at the pentagon-shaped old dark wood table which belonged to Michael, one I never liked. Our style preferences have always been different. I prefer clean and modern. He still enjoys chunky, old, and dark. We had just begun blending our styles as we had moved in together for the first time – it had only been nine months into our three-year relationship. Staring out the sliding glass doors into what most often was my favorite time of day – dusk, faded striations of blue behind black twisted branches of the pine tree, the backyard with dropped pine needles which we never cleaned up. Our patch of wild in 250 square feet. We had a hammock out there that we would have to clean for the rare occasions when we actually slowed down enough to lay there together. I wish we had done more of that now; we never laid there again.

This is when I started an odd relationship with time and numbers. I noticed many odd details I never paid attention to. It started while cooking. I called Michael at 7:47 p.m. and got his voicemail and told him I was making dinner and asked if he could let me know when he would be home. I knew he was riding his bike somewhere, and I didn't know what trail he was on. A few months prior he called me in the middle of my workday to tell me he had decided to go for a bike ride on the Hall Ranch trail in Lyons, he said – just wanted to let you know in case something should happen. I scrawled "Hall Ranch" on the brown paper covering the art table I was using while seeing clients in my private psychotherapy practice. Did he know on some level what was to happen a few months later? I get an eerie feeling when I think about it now. Also, that same eeriness comes over me, remembering an odd feeling of fear I had when we moved into our condo on Thanksgiving weekend of 2011. It had three levels, thus many staircases. I had this irrational sense of fear like I was going to fall down the stairs or fall in the shower and give myself a bad injury. Did I know on some level what was about to happen? Did we both sign up for this even before we became incarnate beings in this lifetime? That's a whole other book...

At 8:09 p.m., I got that pang of sudden sadness while cooking and had to sit down. I called again at 8:47 p.m. and told him I was going to eat without him. While attempting to eat I started googling, "How to report a missing person." I'm extremely grateful for one of the Google searches because it stated clearly: "The myth of waiting 24 hours is bullshit – a lot can happen in two hours, as soon as you know your loved one is missing, make the call."

Finally, at 11:04 p.m., I placed the dreaded call. I don't know why I waited so long. Maybe because I didn't want to make the call. Yet I knew something was very, very wrong as it wasn't like Michael to not respond to my calls and texts. I kept expecting to read or hear this: "Hey honey, I am going to be late tonight, I am sitting in my car talking with my sister which is long overdue. Be home in 45."

While on the first call, I felt the world beginning to spin. This new reality started to set its course. I said out loud to myself, "I can't believe I am making this kind of call." I never imagined having to report a loved one missing. I felt the shock beginning to set up camp in my body – the feeling of being in my body but not wanting to be. The feeling of not wanting this to be my reality and yet it was very much my real life.

I made that call to the non-emergency police line and told the woman my boyfriend hadn't come home and the last thing I knew he was going for a mountain bike ride by himself up near Lyons. She asked me a bunch of questions – what kind of car does he drive? What was the license plate number (no idea!)? What did Michael look like, how tall, and how much did he weigh? I guessed and was correct, except for the license plate – who knows their partner's license plate numbers? After taking my info she said she would call me back.

She called back quickly to tell me I needed to call the Sheriff because Lyons was considered Boulder County, not city. I immediately called the Boulder County Sheriff's office and spoke to Deputy Richard Peebles. That phone number has been ingrained in my brain like a tattoo. His voice was deep and calm. Just talking to him helped calm my nervous system which was beginning to wire itself into a whole new complex pattern. He asked me the same questions. And he knew the Hall Ranch trail well because he asked me, "What parking lot was his car at?" Shit! I didn't know there were two! I had no idea it was so complicated. I didn't know. He said in his calm voice, "I will start at the most used parking lot first and see what we get." He called me again later around 11:40 p.m. just to make sure he had all the correct info as he was about to go out of cellphone range. And then I waited...

I hung up the phone. I stood in my nakedness, only a t-shirt on. I attempted to sleep. I walked through the motions to go to bed. I didn't take my nightly shower because I didn't want to miss the call from them so I hyper-vigilantly pretended I was going to bed. I brushed my teeth, washed my face, put my pajamas on, got into bed, and pulled the covers over me. I turned out the light, but inside I was as lit up as ER lights in an examination room. I knew I couldn't receive the sweet relief of slumber. Not now. I began a new relationship with nighttime, sleep, dreams, my body, and everything I knew; slowly everything started to turn upside down.

At about 1:15 a.m. someone from dispatch called to tell me, "They found him – he is breathing, lucid, and talking." I asked if they could tell me what happened and they said, all I was told to tell you is, "He's breathing, he's lucid, he's talking." And then they said they would call when they were down from the trail.

After the call, I sat on my knees on my white fluffy wool rug and felt a sudden sense of relief to know he was alive but angry and confused because I didn't know what had happened. I was angry for a moment thinking – what did you do to yourself, Michael? I had to come back to feeling relieved he was breathing, lucid, and talking. Those words became like a mantra or prayer, and I repeated them over and over in my mind. And of course, he is talking – if anyone knows Michael, they know he loves to talk and tell stories. I smiled to myself thinking about what he may be telling the EMTs on the mountain.

I am very grateful for Richard Peebles. Much later he told me he believed me even when his supervisor asked, "Are you sure we need to send three rescue crews up there?"

In my voice, Richard could hear the still panic, the sense of impending doom, the sound of something very wrong. It sounds like eerie silence yet with a tiny, stifled scream at the same time. It sounds like a deep, clear knowing voice with a touch of fear and a plea – please help me. It sounds like confusion...trying to calm all the 'what if' characters in my head who suddenly joined me at the dinner table, dinner half-eaten, going down the rabbit hole called Facebook, me frozen and beginning to crack. All the characters joined me, spitting out chicken bones...some of them were getting very angry at Michael for staying out so late.

Yelling their scenarios of what had happened, I believed only one of them, the one that was calm and didn't eat anything. She had a look of shock on her face, she looked as if she had been sitting around a campfire for days. She smelled like ash and fire. She had deep clear eyes, wise from experience and time. She had lived through a lot. Not looking at me and all the other characters around the table, she simply said, "He broke both of his legs, and you will now go get him and bring him home."

Around 2:00 a.m. someone from dispatch called to tell me he was being taken to Longmont United Hospital and Michael wanted me to meet him there. I remember asking in my shocked state, "Will I be able to see him because I am just his girlfriend?" Part of me was thinking about HIPAA rules and guidelines and they wouldn't let me see him because we weren't legally married. I feel bad about that, but I was in shock.

After the call, I was standing in our guest bedroom and stared blankly out the window into the no longer peaceful summer night. Trauma is strange because the worst nightmare is happening, yet the world simply goes on as usual. The night felt calm and peaceful – crickets were singing in that amazing way they just go on and on. I, on the other hand, was starting to feel very bizarre inside – trauma and grief, good old buddies, setting up permanent residence in my system.

I stood there thinking, what do I take with me? What do I wear? My brain felt stuck and overwhelmed by these questions. I defaulted to my favorite old pair of comfortable size six jeans, a t-shirt, and my black hoodie with holes in the pockets and tattered wrists. I put on my comfy clothes that felt like dear old friends, put on my long, somewhat curly blondish hair in a loose ponytail, and grabbed my water bottle, my eyeglasses, and my purse. I remember questioning – do I need a cell phone charger? Nah...I am just going to go pick him up and bring him home, right? I went with hardly anything.

I had sent an email late that night to my dear friend Linda, telling her Michael hadn't come home after his mountain bike ride. I had known Linda the longest since moving to Boulder, Colorado in 1997.

We became instant friends when I answered her ad for housemates, and I was pulled in when it said – interest in music and gardening a plus. I had moved to Boulder to start my graduate studies to become an art therapist at Naropa University, and Linda was in the music therapy program.

Linda checked her email before going to bed and called me around midnight and asked if I wanted her to come over. I told her I was okay. Later, after I got the call where they said he was breathing, lucid, and talking, I told her I was on my way to the hospital, and she asked me, "Do you want me to come with you?"

Without thinking much, I said, "No, I'll be fine."

Actually, I was not fine; and little did I know what was awaiting me. I imagined it was something of much less gravity, just two broken legs and I was going to bring him home. I was in shock and didn't know it yet. Shock is strange, even if it had been two broken legs, I wouldn't have been able to bring him home.

In the ER, I was escorted to a tiny room. It was about 8 x 10 feet and had no windows. On the walls were soothing pictures of Colorado mountains and wildflowers. The furniture, a small loveseat, and four chairs, side tables with bedside table lamps. The furniture was compact and uncomfortable, typical of hospital furniture found in almost every waiting area. Made to be uncomfortable as if they don't want you to set up camp in the waiting area, yet people always do. They should have plush recliners with built-in massagers, but they don't. I was only in there for a short while alone and then a nurse came to sit with me. She was my nurse advocate and was assigned to me. I remember thinking, well, that's strange, why would I have a nurse specifically assigned to me? She asked if I knew someone who could come and be with me. I knew it was bad when she finally just said clearly like a demand, "Call your friend and have her come." I was thinking to myself – it is the middle of the night!

My call to Linda was short. I simply told her I was ordered for her to come be with me. She simply said, "I'm on my way."

When my nurse found out my friend was on her way, she finally told me that Michael had broken his neck. I felt the world stop, and I struggled to breathe. I felt confused, panicked, and just blank like I couldn't comprehend what she had said...he broke his neck? What do you mean? My inner voice who smelt like fire and ash, told me he had only broken both legs which was why he couldn't walk down off the trail. I am simply here to take him home. I couldn't understand it, yet now I knew why she had demanded I have my friend come.

Linda arrived thirty minutes later with a look of love and concern on her face. We embraced and I simply said these four awful words, "He broke his neck." She was now in shock with me as we sat in the room together, quiet and holding hands huddled together. My assigned nurse came in to update us on Michael's condition – he was getting an MRI, and then we heard code blue on the intercom and the nurse ran off. It was suddenly very quiet, and I remember thinking, this is bad, this is very bad. Is he dying right now? Will I even get to see him?

The nurse returned later, and I have no recollection of how long it was as time started a funny relationship with me. It either felt really quick or extremely long and sometimes both at the same time. She told us without any emotion because it's her job and she delivers news like this daily...she said, "He's fine, his heart stopped for a bit, but they revived him and he is now being prepped for neck surgery."

She then introduced me to these two men from the Victim's Compensation Program. Who they worked for, I have no idea. Could have been the Hospital or Boulder County. I never did figure it out. They came to sit with us as standard protocol for trauma. They sat down in the stuffy small room and began telling us cheesy comments like, 'This is going to be really hard.' I so wanted to simply punch them in the face and tell them to fuck off and get out of here, but I didn't. I wanted to yell at them, "Well, of course, this is going to be fucking hard, but I certainly don't need you in here now in this tiny room to tell me that! Get the fuck out of here!" I didn't find their protocoled presence helpful. I didn't need to be told this was going to be hard by total strangers, I simply needed to feel the hand of Linda who was sitting beside me.

I finally got to see Michael after the MRI and before he went to surgery. By this time, it was about 8:00 a.m. The never-ending day kept going. The nightmare I wanted to wake up from. When I first saw him, he was being prepped for surgery and about to be delivered to the operating room. Seeing him for the first time was bizarre. I was in shock, I felt mute, and I felt like there was a wall I wanted to claw through that came up between me and his body. It had something to do with this sense of panic about me not wanting this to be my reality! He saw me. He muffled through the oxygen mask over his mouth, his eyes reaching for me in panic, and said, "I'm really fucked up!"

I shook my head up and down while looking at his body, and I said, "Yes, yes you are. Oh, you have sand all over your face."

He said, "You should see my chest! I was doing ceremony and it was getting dark..." And then we were interrupted by about ten people all prepping him for surgery. They began to hustle and yell. One guy interrupted me and asked me for my name and phone number. I knew they were about to wheel him away to surgery so in my shock I abruptly blurted out, "You don't have to choose this life if you don't want to." And then I told him while looking directly and intensely into his beautiful blue eyes while the hospital staff was buzzing with busyness around us, "I love you. I love you. I love you."

They whisked him off and I looked at my friend and Somatic Therapy mentor, Annie – how did she get here? I wondered why they let her in this prep room before me. I don't remember any of this. Well, after all the hospital staff left us behind like a cloud of dust, I looked at Annie and asked her to sit on me. I needed her to sit on me because I needed her weight to ground me from all the trauma. She sat on top of me, and I cried out, "Annie, wake me up, wake me up!"

And she simply said, "Honey, this is real." And I then wailed and made guttural painful sounds I haven't made since.

Who's Annie and why was she sitting on me? Annie Brook is an amazing psychotherapist who is highly skilled in perinatal psychology and nervous system support. I studied with her for about three years to become a somatic therapist which gave me more embodied skills in my psychotherapy practice. In fact, it was Michael who kept bugging me to take her program because he'd gone through it himself and found it invaluable for being a more balanced human.

I was grateful for her presence in the ER, she knew exactly what I needed when I asked her to sit on me. Now I was getting an inside take on what trauma does to the body. Something extraordinary happens when trauma is suddenly on top of your life. Not that Annie was the trauma, but … it's hard to describe just what I was feeling. If my life were a vase, a precious old beautiful vase, then in an instant it was shattered, busted, gone. Just like Michael's neck. He needed the steady hands of the surgeon, and I needed Annie to sit on me.

When trauma happens, your body may respond in a few ways. One of the ways is dissociation. Your body has the intelligence inside to simply detach itself from the trauma and go elsewhere. I could sense this was happening as I was grappling with this reality which I only wanted to be a nightmare. I wanted to simply wake up at the usual time of day with Michael all showered and ready for his day, and a goodbye kiss as he left for work.

But no, instead I was in this cold, way too bright ER prep room with the flurry of activity; left in the dust of the ER staff as they burst through to whisk him off to repair his neck and save his life. I was left behind as they rolled him away with Annie sitting on me now. I could feel my reality busting me in the inners of my body, I could feel a sense of being shattered from the inside. It's like someone attempting to claw her way out. It's like someone trying to hold on to something so precious and watching it fall to the ground and knowing there was nothing you could do. It was too late.

And *Shock* was now standing beside me. I realized the woman who believed he had broken both of his legs...she was *Shock*. She has survived many "trauma dramas" and what I mean by this is the drama of an awful medical experience that you or your loved one has gone through. It is complex because it is multi-layered with many losses.

Shock looks as still as a morning lake – calm waters with clear reflections. But when you look closer or feel her from the inside, she is a rapid yet slow and steady earthquake. She is shaking from the inside. Bones trying to remain motionless. Muscles and nerves and fascia all were moving a mile a minute, shaking so fast it looks like stillness.

What else does *Shock* look like? She is tall and lanky, skinny and toned from too much activity and too much uncontrollable and spontaneous shaking. This tiny earthquake takes over from deep within her system. Michael's body did this too on the surgery prep table, body void of movement and sensation yet shaking rapidly like his nervous system was trying to savor the way his body used to move. It was in complete and total shutdown and yet very "on." It was as if he was stuck motionless yet at the same time moving 200 mph in one place. *Shock* tries to move but is rooted to one spot. Spinning out and trying to escape the "trauma drama." *Shock* has dark black-brown eyes, bloodshot and empty, yet alive with a panic that is hard to see. Silent alarms, silent screams trying to leak out.

Annie suggested I go home and try to sleep during his 8–10 hour surgery. But that didn't happen. I couldn't sleep for along with *Shock*, comes a full-on adrenaline rush. She shows up sleek, dressed in black leather, ready to run for miles on next to nothing. She can go all day and through the night. She doesn't need sleep medicine. She simply just takes what she thinks is hers – precious cortisol stress hormone to keep her vigilant and hyper-aware mind endlessly active. She hates to wait as she is in constant motion. She gets very angry when she has to stop at red lights. She runs through them to get where she is needed. This is what adrenaline is good for...showing up with superpowers when you need her. She doesn't know when to stop though. She doesn't know she needs rest. She doesn't know there is a limit to the cortisol streaming through her blood.

CHAPTER 2

MICHAEL AND ME

"Loving you feels like my commitment to eternity
a long time ago."

—Nicola An

Michael and I met surrounded by red rocks at Ken's Lake Campground near Moab, Utah in 2007. We were camping there with a group to attend the Contact Improvisation Dance Jam. It wasn't love at first sight. It was for him though, I think, but not for me. You see, at that time, I had a different idea of who I thought I was searching for, and I thought I knew just who would make a great match for me. Turns out, I had no idea because actually, it was Michael who was the best for me. But it would take a couple of years for me to realize this.

Michael and I used to dance every Sunday morning, attending what they called "contact improvisation lab." It's a lab because the focus is on both an inner process as well as improving your skills as a dancer and the relationship between the two. And sometimes they lead exercises to help you focus your intention and bring attention to what is happening in your life and how it relates to your dance. They suggest you communicate your needs and boundaries with your other dance partners. It's a practice rich in many ways with metaphors that can be applied to your life as well as your dance.

I feel proud to have met him in the context of Contact Improvisation in the dusty, dry campground. I love this form of dance and the community it blesses me with. It still blesses me even though I don't dance nearly as much as I used to. Contact Improvisation, often referred to as "contact improv" or "CI" for short, is a dance form that uses a rolling point of contact between you and the floor, your constant dance companion, and your other partners – could be one person or a few. It uses a give-and-take of weight exchange with another. It is physics in motion. It's addictive, well at least for me, it's like giving and getting a massage at the same time. It's an exquisite embodiment practice and it grounds me unlike anything else. Remember when I mentioned how I wanted my friend Annie to sit on me in the emergency room as they took Michael off for surgery? Well, she is part of my contact community and when the shock took hold of me, my body needed to feel Annie's weight. I needed this to know where I was in time and space. I needed both her touch and her weight to stay grounded and to stay in my body.

Michael and my relationship grew within this dance community, the seed was planted when we met in that campground in beautiful Moab, and it grew with us and held us together. Partnerships need community. After dating for a year, we asked the community to honor us at CI lab. For birthdays, you can request to be lifted and held by the group while being sung to and carried throughout the room. Well, for our anniversary, the community lifted us as a couple! He was on the bottom, and I was on top, we were held up in an embrace while also being held by the community. It was a beautiful moment in time, and when I remember it, the healing power of our community drenches my heart.

When I first met Michael, I was living in Denver working as a counselor at a school for pregnant and parenting teenagers while also working as a contract therapist. My dream was to have a private practice someday. I was 37 at the time and single and had been for most of my adult life. My longest relationship ever had only been six months. I didn't have a great track record with relationships. Michael admitted he had red flags about my lack of long-term relationships when he first started dating me. He'd been married once before and when I met him, he was three years out from his divorce. He shared years later that he almost left our relationship a few times, but every time he thought of this, he'd hear a strong message from Spirit for him to stay. He listened and remained.

Dating wasn't easy for me because I didn't see the huge red flags all around me with my first serious relationship at the innocent and naïve age of 19. I was studying abroad in Mexico for my junior year of college and was getting an unofficial education in toxic relationships although I didn't know it. I was blinded to the fact that the relationship was abusive in many ways – emotionally, mentally, sexually, and physically. That relationship lasted only four months, but the trauma of it lasted for decades.

It was ten years later when the blinders came off. I was sitting on a comfortable but old couch, and I had to expend energy to not fall into the person sitting next to me. I was attending a training to work as a children's counselor at a battered women's shelter. The instructor was casually explaining the spectrum of abuse while drawing it all with dry-erase markers on a whiteboard. My eyes were finally opened, and I began to have layers of understanding come to me as I remembered how I was abused in subtle and sneaky ways. I had been gaslit, manipulated, isolated, and more. My confusion lifted in that moment while at the same time, there was a heaviness upon me as I was finally able to say out loud – I was abused and raped by the person I thought I loved.

It took me ten years to even see the toxicity in this first relationship and then it took me another seven years to be able to trust another deeply. I found a therapist with the help of my friend Merryl who I was living with at the time. We laughed a lot and were art therapy classmates. She also saw me struggling and finally spoke up about it. I'd been feeling suicidal because of depression that had roots in this abusive relationship.

She made me sit on my bed in my attic bedroom, the sun was streaming in from the skylight, she stood near me, handed me her phone, and said, "Here this is my therapist's number, call her and make an appointment, you need help, Beth."

She sat next to me while I dialed the number and left a message. I am grateful for this, because without my years of therapy and healing from being held by friends and professionals, I wouldn't have ever found Michael and been able to open my heart to his.

Michael's heart...let me explain why I love him as much as I do. I adore these qualities in him. He's dedicated, sensitive, loving, and deeply curious about everything. He's also the most persistent and downright stubborn person I know, he is, after all, a Taurus. I am so thankful he kept pursuing me. He didn't give up on me even when he really wanted to. And his persistence is one of the qualities I'm attracted to the most.

Michael has had a chronic health issue for half of his life. It's a mysterious yet constant digestion issue. He's devoted time, energy, and a lot of money toward finding a cure and having more ease in his body. In the process, he discovered the best way to take care of himself which included a very strict and limited diet. When we met, he was basically only eating winter squash, zucchini, lettuce, avocados, and all kinds of meat. We were both foodies, so I was amazed at his devotion and willingness to eat such a limited diet.

It wouldn't be until about two years later we started dating and it took some convincing from others. At this time, I was seriously searching for a life partner. I was on this ridiculous challenge from some lady's dating advice about saying yes to anyone who asked you out because you simply don't know who you think would be good for you. She also suggested I do a minimum of 100 first dates with anyone who asked me. When we started dating, I was already dating someone else and saying yes to all offers, which weren't many, but for some reason, I was intent on having as many dates as possible. Ironically, I said no to Michael's dates numerous times because I considered him just a friend. He was also recently divorced and was bitter and angry towards his ex. I saw this as a red flag and decided he wasn't ready for a relationship at that time.

But he was persistent, and he persevered. A few times when he asked me out, I would go, but for some reason, I considered these just hang-out times with a friend. It's funny now because we argue about when our actual first date was. He claims it was the time he was driving through Denver and asked if we could have lunch together. He was traveling back from an osteopathic bodywork training, which is the work he is most passionate about.

He showed up at my quaint, adorable apartment. He brought a roasted chicken, salad, and avocados and we walked to my neighborhood park near the lake, spread a picnic blanket, and ate and talked under the cottonwood trees. It was very romantic, but I was absolutely clueless about this since he was "just a friend" in my mind.

I claim our first date was the time I asked him if he had lunch plans while we were dancing at CI Lab at the Pearl Street studio, with creaky old wood floors. He didn't, so we went to a fancy restaurant with white tablecloths. He denies this was our first date, but I considered it the beginning of our official dating history. This was after three of my very close friends had all suggested, without talking to each other, that I should seriously consider dating Michael. I will never forget the words of my dear friend Jenny, a dance therapist, who said, "You should date Michael, you two are knit from the same cloth."

She was right. And it's a beautiful cloth of deeply rich colored velvets – emerald green, turquoise, cobalt blue, purple, and several reds all sewn together to create a solid patchwork quilt. As you pull it up toward your neck to nestle in and get really warm it comforts you with its soft heaviness.

When I finally surrendered to what my friends were telling me, I took a risk and opened my heart to him and to love. I was blessed with the most amazing man. I finally found my life partner and true companion. I began to learn about myself in new ways that only being in a relationship can teach you. I began to grow from having him as a mirror and ass-kicker in my life. Yes, Michael kindly kicked my ass, not literally, although now we joke and say we would love to have him be able to literally kick me in the ass. His ass-kicking was how he showed me my failings and encouraged me to be a better human. And I do the same for him; we strive to help each other be better human beings and as we like to say, better human "lovings."

Early in our dating life, Michael invited me for a weekend cabin getaway on the St. Vrain River near Fort Collins, Colorado. Being the gentleman he is, he suggested I invite my best friend, Tauna, and her boyfriend to join us. We'd only been dating for a few weeks at that point, and he didn't want it to be awkward or have me think he was jumping the gun.

Tauna had recently moved to Boulder from Hawaii where she'd lived for a decade. Our friendship survived physical separation. She was now working for an Ayurvedic practitioner to hone her skills and had actually studied Ayurveda in India. We met at a full moon gathering when we were in our 20s. And it was love at first sight – we saw each other from across the circle and we each thought to ourselves – Hi, there you are! And we knew we were going to be friends because it felt like we'd already known each other in another lifetime.

And speaking of friends...there's something special and also very unique when you start to date one of them. When I started dating Michael it was a slow burn. I remember wondering if I would be sexually attracted to him. Then, one night in the cozy cabin we were watching the Tom Hanks movie "Big" on an old VHS machine. We sat close on an uncomfortable futon couch; he put his hand on my thigh, and I finally felt the amazing zing of sexual energy rush through my body. I was excited, relieved, and a bit nervous too. I didn't respond in the moment, but in my mind, our budding new relationship was sealed.

We had our first kiss the next morning. We had slept in separate beds, he begrudgingly slept on the futon in the living room, while I was in the bedroom. I didn't want him to sleep with me thinking we wouldn't get any sleep if we did. I asked him to wake me up in the morning. He entered the room and snuggled next to me on top of the covers. Since I didn't respond in any way with his subtle physical advance the night before, he was confused and didn't know how to be with me now. Aware of this, I pulled back the covers dramatically and said, "Get in here!"

That's when we had our first kiss with the wise old cottonwoods, the brilliant Colorado sun, and the St. Vrain River as our witnesses peeking in through the sliding glass door.

Driving home from the weekend in my old tiny dark green Toyota Rav 4 which had originally been my dad's car, this thought came to me suddenly, "I want to support Michael to be the best Michael he can be." This inner knowing seemed to have come from outside of me; it felt as solid and beautiful as a piece of petrified wood. It was almost like a command. It had a sense of purpose and direction. I think this voice came from Spirit or a higher power, God or the Universe. And I wonder if it came from the same source as the voice who kept telling Michael to stay with me. At the time, I remember thinking, well, I've never thought that about anyone I've dated, much less in such a short amount of time in my dating history.

Another "seal of the deal" was when we attended the funeral of the father of one of his best friends. Michael and Mark had been friends for decades, they met in college. I was helping Mark bring out food from the Lutheran church kitchen. A scene I was comfortable in because my father was a Lutheran pastor, as was Mark's father. Yes, I'm a PK, a pastor's kid, or a TO, a theologian's offspring.

Mark and I could see and hear Michael talking passionately about his work with a few people and Mark said to me, "Michael is one high-quality human being. You found a good one."

He was so right, and I made note of it. Hearing comments like these are like getting really good reference letters for a job you really want. I wish there was a way we could ask for references when beginning the process of a relationship. Michael is definitely a high-quality man and human being. It only took me 37 years to find him, and it was well worth the wait!

Michael is one of the most passionate peeps I know. He's passionate about physical health – his and the well-being of others. He has a deep curiosity about everything and this pulled me in because this is a quality I value as well. He's sensitive as hell and is more emotional at times than a menstruating person. He cries easily when his emotions are stirred. He often cries during commercials, movies, YouTube videos, and America's Got Talent. He's most moved by medical miracle stories probably because he has been searching for ease in his body long before his tragic biking accident. He began having mysterious digestive issues in his early 20s which thrust him into a life direction of devoting time and energy toward learning about how the body functions from the inside out. He studied electrical engineering in college and worked for Kodak for a few years. He loved those young adulting days – having money and finding a career path he loved. But then his back went out and he found Rolfing, a form of bodywork focused on the structure of the body. Eventually, he discovered a form of bodywork called Visceral Manipulation or Osteopathic Bodywork where you listen to and work with the body to help realign it. This involves gently working with veins, arteries, and organs and not using pressure or force on the body. When we first started dating, he had recently devoted his entire life to learning this new method. He dove headfirst into full-on dedication. Ironic because the accident also had him dive headfirst into solid rock.

What was he doing up on the trail at dusk anyway? At the time of the accident, Michael had been doing some soul work on his lineage and his life. I had also asked him earlier in the summer to get clear about my request to see if I could get pregnant. I wanted to be a mother, I wanted to birth my own baby. I had searched deep within myself during the winter of 2011 as I had been on the fence about becoming a Mama, and I was going to be turning 42 on August 24th, time was running out. I asked him for his answer by the end of the summer. It was almost the end of August, and I was eager to know.

The accident was the answer. We would not be trying to get pregnant. No, instead our life would be completely turned upside down in a totally different way. I distinctly remember feeling a sense of odd acceptance regarding my desire to be a mother. It was as if a lost puzzle piece had been put into place and then suddenly it all made sense. I felt it viscerally with a knowing in my body that this is why I couldn't see myself birthing and mothering my own child. This was coming.

CHAPTER 3

BACK IN THE ER

"I can't go on, I'll go on."

—Samuel Beckett

What I birthed instead was grief, or rather, grief would be birthing me. Before I explain this, I want you to know more about what Michael and I had to endure. Bear with me loves and keep breathing, we start again on the dreaded first day that seemed to go on forever…

The neurosurgeon sitting in the nurses' station in front of her computer turns around to look up at me. I notice her leg shaking like the shock inside me – very fast, minute shaking motions like she was very angry or seriously jacked up on caffeine. That had to be it because it was very early in the morning, like 4:00 a.m. I remember the scene clearly – her crossed-legged foot wearing dark purple sparkly Dansko clogs shaking too fast, and then her words hit me, and the shock dropped deeper into my system. This was the first time anyone told me anything official about his condition even though I had been escorted into the tiny family room for high dramas such as this. She said to me, "His neck is broken, and the cord severed, he'll most likely be a quadriplegic for the rest of his life."

That awful word bounced around the sides of my skull as I thought to myself—Uh, what? Quadriplegic? Her words felt like they were moving into me as fast as her leg was moving and yet at the same time those words entered slowly like smooth molasses. Because my brain couldn't comprehend it, I turned to the nurse advocate who had been assigned to me and asked, "What does severed mean?"

She simply said, "Severed means cut."

And as she said this, she made scissor motions with her fingers just to drive the meaning in deeper for me as if we were playing the game of rock-paper-scissors. The rock he landed on was winning this game.

I started to spin on the inside and yet I also felt like I couldn't move; it was as if I was stuck in thick honey. It was like I was paralyzed; what I was feeling on the inside was what Michael was experiencing and would feel (or not feel) for the rest of his life. I wanted to hear he'd just broken both his legs, and that he'd be coming home with me. That was what *Shock*, dressed in badass black leather, had told me when I first got the call to meet him at the hospital. But quadriplegia? Quadriplegia? It took me a while to grok what this meant for me and us. My world was continuing to go upside down and now sideways. No one ever plans or even thinks about dealing with quadriplegia or any other 'plegia,' do they? I never did. No one plans for becoming disabled.

Let me explain the difference between quadriplegia also known as tetraplegia, and paraplegia because actually many people assume Michael has more abilities than he does. They assume he is a paraplegic. The Latin root of *para* is two and it only affects the lower limbs, thus a paraplegic has all functions of their arms, wrists, and fingers as well as their core abdominal muscles. *Quad* is Latin for four — which means all four limbs, upper and lower, arms and legs, and usually the torso are all compromised in some way. Every injury is slightly different, for example, one friend of ours who has quadriplegia has the use of his middle finger only…which comes in handy when pissed off or using it as a hook.

The root "plegia" in Greek means to strike or a blow or stroke; it also means paralysis or cessation of motion and sensation. Combine these two root words quad + plegia[1] = a blow to all four limbs. I would say it was a blow to our entire life.

Another aspect of quadriplegia is your loss of motion and sensation depends on not only where the vertebrae are broken, but also how the spinal cord itself is damaged. In the world of quadriplegia, the term complete or incomplete is used like "C5 complete" or "C4 incomplete." (C stands for cervical as in your cervical spine, C-0 is at the base of your skull).

It sounds black and white, but it isn't. It's many shades of gray. The average size of the spinal cord is about 14mm in diameter which is just a breath over a half inch. Michael's spinal cord was almost completely severed; he only had about a millimeter left. Spinal cord injury is complicated as we would soon learn. That tiny moment in time tumbled us into a crash course of learning about all things related to the world of quadriplegia and disability. We were hanging on by one small millimeter like a rock climber holding onto a tiny ledge to propel upwards.

The spinal cord is miraculous! Do you know all it does for you? It's the communication system of the body; it's like telephone wires sending millions of messages to the big boss – the brain. It's our interstellar system full of neurotransmitters; like shooting stars in the night sky, like the Milky Way carrying messages to the source. It reminds me of one of my favorite paintings by Georgia O'Keefe called *The Lawrence Tree*. With the colors maroon, black, dark blue, and white, she captures the view looking up into the night sky through the silhouette of a tall ponderosa pine tree. The tree is surrounded by the night sky full of bright stars. Is this what Michael saw as he lay there for hours staring up at the night sky waiting to be rescued?

---

[1] The same meaning is tied to the root of the slang word "Fuck." Fuck v. To blow, to hit, to strike. Dutch origin. I learned this in the Netflix documentary called *History of Swear Words*.

It was far from what I was looking at in the dimly lit nurses' station early that morning. More and more staff began to arrive and were beginning to bustle around, hushed conversations and prepping for their day. I stared into the neurosurgeon's computer screen to see the evidence of the dreaded word quadriplegia. The facts I didn't want to see were true. She let me peer into the monitor and showed me where his vertebrae bones were shattered – C3 through C7 with C5 completely destroyed and broken into bits. Remember how I said Michael heard the crunching sounds of dura and bones breaking? Well, I now had a visual black-and-white proof.

My eyes locked on the x-ray of brokenness, the evidence of what was, what is, and what will be, I stood there frozen and in shock; again, I felt paralyzed. Even with the x-ray evidence, my mind just couldn't grok it. My mind was flooded with questions like – are you sure the spinal cord is severed? Are you sure there's only a millimeter left? Can't you simply just sew it back together? Isn't there some sort of special medical miracle glue to return it to its normal state of amazingness?

Knowing our life was to be incredibly difficult and that Michael's losses were immense, I had told him he didn't have to choose this life. I didn't want him to feel obligated to stay for me or anyone else. I didn't want him to stay for this kind of life if he didn't want to. He never responded. He couldn't with the oxygen mask on amidst the flurry of activity as they wheeled him away. His system was compromised big time. There were so many things going wrong with his body physically and medically.

Eventually, after surgery we would learn this: C5 was blasted. His spinal cord was severed. One of his arteries was crushed and he had internal bleeding in his neck. They implanted screws and rods to stabilize it. Before the surgery he was having difficulty breathing due to the location of the break in his neck – it was impacting the nerves that control his breathing and possibly swallowing. While they were giving him an MRI last night his heart stopped, he had a 3-minute heart attack, and they had to give him CPR. They may have broken a rib.

Yes, Michael was indeed "fucked up," which were the words he uttered to me when I first saw him, with C5 completely shattered, destroyed, gone, and C4 also partly compromised. This was catastrophic as this part of the spinal cord sends communication directly to the lungs and is also connected to the thyroid gland, heart, diaphragm, vertebral arteries, trachea, and esophagus.

The surgery was a serious rebuild. They built a cage to replace his vertebra out of titanium rods and screws and mixed some of the remaining bits of original bone with some kind of medical goo. (There was a special kind of glue, but not one to bring your spinal cord back to normal.) This goo would combine with his bits of bone and C5 would eventually grow back. At least this is what I remember being told by the anesthesiologist. He was tall, dressed in scrubs, and had those glasses with special X-ray lenses propped up on his forehead. When he saw my perplexed face, he said, "Here, would you like me to draw it instead? It'd be easier to explain if I do it that way. Could I see your booklet?"

Before he even finished speaking, I eagerly gave it to him. A drawing was much easier for my brain to comprehend because I was overwhelmed; grief and trauma brain is real. He drew the diagram of Michael's neck cage and explained it while he drew. He drew this in my little orange notebook I happened to have in my purse at the time. It goes from a simple regular life list of things to buy – balloons, a plant stand, a feather duster, to notes from the doctor about his condition. Learning about how they rebuilt his neck felt like a scene out of a sci-fi laboratory, well, really this is what modern medicine can be at times, freakish yet amazing. Our life definitely was freakish. Here let me show you the full list:

-Spinal cord shredded from bone fragments

-Graft and plate in C4-C7, drains in front and back (C=cervical spine)

-Removal of C4-C5 (vertebra bones)

-Blood loss 1600cc

-Spinal cord is compressed

-Swelling C3-C6

-Neurogenic pulmonary edema (lungs filled with fluid)

-Heart is irregular; very difficult to control; on meds; doesn't appear to have any damage.

-Left all bone on back, left screws C3-C6, right screws-C4, C5, C6; these are like suspenders

-Cadaver bone in back wrapped in material; bone should grow around it

-Titanium screws and rods should last – won't get pulled out or torn because he won't be moving

-Sedated with meds for lung fluid, and irregular heartbeat, this could change when he can breathe on his own

-Left vertebral artery (dominant) injured, no blood to C2-C5

-Artery on right is helping, but could get clotted, high risk of stroke

-Can't give him an anti-coagulant (why?)

-6-inch incision on front and back of neck; staples on back, tape on front

-Antibiotics to prevent pneumonia

-He has all known complications

Yes, Michael did indeed have all known complications. And he'd have even more eventually. He'd be in the ICU for quite a while. I began to count the days after day five as they all seemed to run together like a bad watercolor painting. My life had suddenly become distinctly divided into pre- and post-accident, like a knife splitting wood, or cutting a baby's umbilical cord, or a bone cutting through a spinal cord…

A lot happened in those first few days, well, actually, the entire first year. Let me try to summarize it, but how do you summarize medical trauma drama succinctly? Let me try explaining it in numbers like from the line from my favorite Rent song, *Seasons of Love*, where the chorus is about counting all the amazing moments like sunsets and cups of coffee.

If we do this with trauma drama it would go something like this. It all started in a split second when he hit one rock. He waited about 5 hours and 15 minutes to be found by three rescue crews. It took them 95 minutes to find him and about 45 minutes to get him down off the trail and to the nearest hospital which was 11.1 miles away.

His surgery prep took about 2 hours, or did it? The time between when I arrived there and when the ten people in the ER crew wheeled him away for surgery is a blur for sure. What was I doing for almost six hours?

He had one neurosurgeon and one anesthesiologist. He had a rotation of about four nurses; he'd have two or three per day and one at night. He'd have more CNAs (certified nurse assistants). CNAs deal with everything coming out of the body – shit, pee, puke, lung, and other body part goo; and nurses put things in – meds, needles, catheters, etc. Now you know the difference.

His surgery lasted about eight hours. How can neurosurgeons do that? They are an entirely different breed of people. Are they really just aliens? Post-surgery Michael seemed alien. He was connected to two machines, one to monitor his heart and the other to his lungs. He was attached to two IV drips – one for saline and the other for a high dose of pain meds. He was tired and extremely still. Yes, his body was eerily still; he was no longer full of intense tiny, minute shaking motions as he was when I first saw him right after they brought him in, then his body was still shaking off the trauma to his system

No, now he was motionless, like a still lake. The room was eerily quiet yet alive with many disturbing noises; it was beeping and buzzing with all the machines keeping him alive, but it was also a buzz with trauma, grief, and disbelief. It's ironic, what he needed most was rest and the environment was the very opposite of this. Hospitals are the worst place for getting any kind of sleep or rest. There are constant interruptions. Constant sounds of machines cycling with meds and fluids, and a breathing apparatus. His lungs were not working on their own. He was wired to a ventilator to assist with his breathing. He had a tube down his throat to make him breathe. Modern medicine was keeping him alive as he was simply struggling to survive.

It's a miracle he even survived, thanks to the rescue crews and modern medicine. Without these, he would have been dead. We were in the ICU for 45 days. His situation was complex; we began to set up camp in the ICU. Some of us slept there. We stayed there as much as we could. Our community would bring us food. We took over the waiting room kitchen. I felt like I got to know the hospital staff and volunteers really well. Friendships I would have preferred to never have had.

Our life was upside down with me navigating a sudden 180-degree turn of life as I knew it and Michael simply fighting to stay alive. He was all over the map with blood pressure issues. He was mostly low and passing out a lot. The doctors and nurses were experimenting with medications to help stabilize him. It was trial and error, mostly error. At some point, I came to the conclusion the hospital staff knew very little about how to care for someone with acute quadriplegia.

A few days after the surgery a nurse who was a walking encyclopedia of spinal cord injuries showed up on one of his shifts. She reassured us and told us the "new normal" might not be stabilized until a year from now...and this is normal. (I've discovered it never feels normal, well it does but doesn't. It takes longer than a year for any of this to ever feel normal. One year is a very short amount of time in the world of quadriplegia.) With her sudden appearance, I began to feel paranoid. Why, all of a sudden does the hospital have an expert in SCI? Did they find her just for us so we wouldn't sue them? Where the fuck was she when he was first admitted? It felt really weird to feel paranoid like I didn't trust the world anymore; I no longer felt safe, I even felt paranoid with some of my friends who were offering their opinions and advice.

Looking back, I see we were all distraught, and offering advice was a way to cope with the helplessness we were all feeling. Trauma drama comes hand in hand with helplessness. And grief comes with many other losses…like my loss of trusting myself and the world.

During surgery, I wanted to be a fly on the wall, I mean, how does one reconstruct a neck? What does the operating table look like? Did they somehow flip him like a pancake to get to the back of his neck? He had two incisions, one on the back side about 5 inches long starting at the bottom of his neck up to the base of his skull, it's like Frankenstein – a line up the middle with dots on either side. And he has another incision on the left side of his neck in the front.

He almost died from a heart attack when he coded blue before surgery which was the only time I thought he could die. I never fully let this in because *Shock* wouldn't let me really feel it. And it's wild because he was actually very close to death; in fact, death was cuddling with him. I believe part of me was very aware of this and yet another part of me needed to tuck the morbid thought away in order to be strong for myself, Michael, and others. I became very aware of the present moment, all those years of meditating, and here I was crystal clear and hyper-aware of each second. In a way it was a beautiful gift delivered with skull and crossbones wrapping paper; except I didn't see the skull and crossbones. I was in survival mode for myself, I was in denial and perhaps felt an intuitive hit he was going to survive somehow. Whatever it was, I realize now I needed to do this so I could deal with what was actually happening in my life. To deal with reality, I had to believe in my hopeful fantasy he was going to live, even if it meant living with quadriplegia.

Yes, while death was cuddling with Michael, quadriplegia was taking a firm seat in my lap. I still don't want it in my life…it's like one of those shits where no matter how many times you wipe yourself you can't get clean, so you end up peeling off all your clothes and hopping in the shower. But with this, however, you cannot clean it off of yourself… this shit-show called quadriplegia. I really do hate that word. I couldn't even spell it right in the beginning; looking back in my journal on my computer you will see quadriplegia underlined with red dots of error. I left it that way, it made sense because it's just wrong; and very fucked up.

This dreaded first day went on forever because I hadn't slept and it felt like I was inside an unending nightmare. Annie suggested I take a break and go back to our three-story condo and try to get some rest since I'd been there since 2:00 a.m. I attempted to take a nap in our bed, but I was too sad and overwhelmed to lay there without him, knowing I'd most likely never sleep with him there again. I moved to the floor to lay on my wool rug instead, but my body wouldn't let me sleep, so I took a long hot shower instead. But that just made me even more sad because I thought of Michael the entire time. He would never shower there again; he would never stand up in the shower stall and feel the sweet and simple pleasure of warm water running down his body. I cried for him and myself. Just a few months prior we had placed plastic on the huge bathroom skylight to keep the heat in and at the last minute, I threw confetti up there for something silly. He loved this addition to our bathroom decor. He loved this playful part of me which would become a source of strength for me, for Michael, and for many others in the coming months.

This part of me was very subdued seeing him for the first time after surgery. I don't remember it exactly. I was in the hospital room where I felt like a stranger, the room felt alien to me as he was hooked up to medical devices of all kinds. He didn't seem human amongst all the tubes and machines keeping him alive. Rhonda, his mama bear nurse, came into the room and saw me just standing there staring at Michael. She looked as if she could retire soon and was short, stocky, and round, and I just wanted her to hug me.

She said in an overly cheerful voice, "Do you want me to wake him up?"

I hesitated.

She continued, "It would be good for him to know you're here."

I wasn't sure this would be allowed, and I was wondering if he'd be in too much pain. But I did want him to know I was there holding him, supporting and loving him. He was so drugged up on pain meds, he was in a deep sleep.

I nodded yes while I stared at his drugged-up post-surgery state as I could feel *Shock* in my system getting more and more comfortable.

She simply said, "I'll stop it, he's on the med Michael Jackson was addicted to, it's called 'white lightning' and it's super strong stuff, gets the job done. It'll only take about 30 seconds and he'll wake up. I'll just do it quick so he knows you're here."

She stopped the drip of pain meds. It took a bit for him to open his beautiful blue eyes to see me. I waited nervously to see him come to consciousness. As his eyes opened, I could feel him reaching for me through his eyes, and he had both a look of panic and relief; yes, panic and relief at the same time. This was the beginning of our relationship of holding the rich experience of both, the bitter and the sweet. On the one hand, I saved you...and on the other hand...I saved you for this? This became a common theme in our life.

He couldn't talk to me because of the breathing tube in his throat. I touched his head but was afraid to touch him in the alien post-surgery state and I wasn't sure he could feel me, and I didn't want to hurt him even more. I touched his head often thinking it might be the only place he could feel me touching him. And I wanted him to know I was there.

I vaguely remember what I said to him. I had to hold back all my questions; they were like eager shoppers waiting to enter the stores on Black Friday. Questions like— what the hell happened, what do you remember, how do you feel, and what can you feel? But I only said what truly mattered, "I'm here Michael. I love you."

And we simply looked into each other's teary and wide-open eyes for about 30 seconds.

Then nurse Rhonda started the constant drip of white lightning back into his veins as we both could tell he was in excruciating pain. I didn't want to see him suffer yet seeing him lying there was full of nothing but suffering for all of us.

CHAPTER 4

GRIEF RIPPLES OUT

*"It is natural that people around you start to grieve when you do.
We know that when you have pain it's not a personal pain, it is a
pain of the whole group. We experience a collective sharing so that an
individual doesn't need to bear all the weight of the suffering."*

—Sobonfu Somé

This tragedy didn't happen to just the two of us but to his family and mine, and our entire community. The tragic news spread like wildfire. With the first being our families. At some point around 4:00 a.m., my nurse advocate asked me if I wanted to call his parents. They were living in Maine at the time, so it'd only be 6:00 a.m. I remember thinking, I don't want to make this call and be the giver of news that will change their lives forever. I don't want to hear their voices crack with sorrow and disbelief. I asked her to call them for me. I also thought to myself – I want them to enjoy their lives before their world is turned upside down. Have you ever had to be the bearer of bad news such as this? I wanted them to enjoy a bit more of their pre-accident life because it would never be the same.

I did call my parents just before 6:00 a.m. And I'll never forget hearing their emotional disbelief. My dad answered the phone. He sensed something was wrong, I'm not a morning person and I never call them early to simply chat and say hi. I spoke in short sentences like a toddler who's just learned to put words together.

I simply said, "Hi Dad. I'm in the ER."

"What?" My Dad's voice cracked with confusion and shock. Like the word couldn't escape his throat, as if it got stuck partially in his vocal cord. No matter how hard you try, it's a sound you simply cannot repeat, but I can hear it as if it was yesterday.

"Michael crashed on his mountain bike. He broke his neck. He may be a quadriplegic. They're prepping him for surgery now."

I could hear my mom alert and getting out of bed and beginning to ask my dad a bunch of questions. She's a retired post-operation nurse and she's always ready for action when a loved one is hurt. My parents are amazing. They live two hours away in Colorado Springs, and there was simply no question as my mom said, "We're on our way" with a strong clear knowing.

I felt their support immediately knowing they were on their way. They arrived at 8:00 a.m. I met them at the front entrance outside near the main parking lot. We stood there awkwardly in the beautiful sunshine. We didn't say much, they simply embraced me, and we cried huddled together. It would have been fine if the sun hadn't risen to meet me. My life was dark, very dark and the light was annoying and didn't make any sense, I mean, how could the sun be shining as bright as it was? By now it was August 28th, another beautiful late summer day, and I hated it. I was dumbfounded by this new upside-down world I suddenly found myself in.

As soon as Michael's parents, Armand and Bonnie, and his sister Linda and her husband, Greg, heard the news, they immediately made arrangements to come and arrived later around midnight. I met them at the ER entrance and escorted them through the maze of a hospital. Like in many hospitals, after hours you had to enter through the ER, and I already knew how to get to Michael's room even though I'd been there less than 24 hours. The ICU was becoming my new home away from home. Seeing his family arrive in the florescent overly lit hallway, I could clearly see grief, sorrow, pain, and pure exhaustion on their faces. They had come directly from the airport and had been traveling all day.

They rushed down the hall to meet me dragging their rolling suitcases behind them. We hugged quickly and kept moving because they needed to see Michael before they settled in for the night. His dad briefly said to me, "We had hoped to have come out here for a very different occasion."

And we all knew what he was referring to —a wedding, as Michael and I were getting closer to such an endeavor. Actually, the accident was becoming a strange kind of elopement, a very different kind of wedding. Michael described it once like this – our hearts were squished together in a way only trauma can do.

If the accident was our unofficial wedding ceremony…then I guess it made his long stay in the ICU our unique honeymoon. Yes, he was in the ICU for 45 days or sixty-four thousand eight hundred minutes. Google told me the average length of stay in the ICU is just 3.3 days with a 1½ day stay in a post-operation room. This brings me back to numbers and to try to explain all this succinctly. I'm aware I could go down the rabbit hole of endless details because there are many.

He was in a complex and compounded situation. His lungs were compromised big time. Remember all the key processes C4 and C5 do for the body? Basically, anything having to do with his throat and neck was challenged. He had had a few respiratory arrests. He almost died a few times in the ER, and once or twice in the operating room or prep room.

Recovery was brutal; he was in a lot of pain. He was on massive doses of pain meds and had a tube in his mouth which meant he couldn't speak, nor could he breathe on his own. He was on many medications – at least six. One was to keep his blood pressure up and one was to manage the pain, and I can't remember what the rest were for.

He had lots of visitors who wanted to see him. We had to turn many away. His team of nurses and doctors limited visitors because he really just needed to rest. Only one or two people were allowed in at a time.

And my phone was blowing up with texts and emails with messages of love and healing and questions about his condition. I was amazed at how many loving and concerned messages I started receiving. Each message was a balm to my shattered soul reminding me to keep going. I tried to write simple messages back but was overwhelmed and just couldn't. I wish my phone had the limited visitor's policy like the ICU did, as it was too much to get back to everyone. I was relieved when our two best friends, Tauna and Mark, volunteered to set up a Lotsa Helping Hands website to update them on his process and to remind them not to visit. When help arrived, I gratefully said yes. It would be the beginning of me gracefully saying yes often when help was offered.

After just two hours of this website being live, Michael already had more than 300 people tuning in. He had many connections from his childhood to his college days to his professional life at Kodak and then most recently in Fort Collins and the dance CI community.

I began to have a new routine for my days. I would wake up early, after not sleeping the best, and have breakfast – cereal, with my coffee in a to-go mug. Then I'd drive straight to the hospital. I never slept there as I needed to get my rest, which was easier in my own bed even though there was a stark emptiness of Michael missing. I would try to arrive at the hospital early to hear the doctor's reports. I would mostly miss them because they usually made their rounds before 6:00 a.m. I'd stay as long as possible, then if I had clients that day, I would drive to either my Boulder or Denver offices. I imagined the line on the map as a way to stay connected to him. His place in the hospital became my central point. And if you would draw all my driving routes there and back, it would look like some kind of weird abstract flower.

I began paying attention to numbers as I began to see double digits everywhere—my clocks and the odometer in my car. They kept me connected to Michael, feeling as though it was a message from Spirit – we were together, and our love was strong. There was one time on my commute – on the busy Denver I-25 when I glanced to my right and saw a disturbing ad on the side of a bus – it was a photo of a mountain biker falling midair. I was stunned and then super pissed. And I wanted to call and complain about it, but I had many other things drawing my attention, the main one being Michael's well-being. I never did call to complain; I had to choose my battles wisely.

After seeing clients I'd come straight back to the hospital to be with Michael. I would drive home late and then decompress by writing for about 45 minutes to an hour. My writing became a nightly ritual as I wrote updates about his condition and his progress. It became a balm for me and a way to contain and process the enormity of the situation. And it connected me to others through many daily supportive emails. I'd finally turn out the lights and try to get some sleep around midnight or later.

In those beginning few days, a lot happened, and I wrote many updates. Right after the surgery and for the first few days of post-op he was intubated, which means he had a tube stuffed down his throat to assist with his breathing since he couldn't breathe on his own. This tube was connected to the ventilator which also meant he couldn't talk.

The hospital staff gave us something they called the "Superboard." Why they call it a fucking superboard, I have no idea. Basically, a superboard is a letter chart – it's the alphabet. It should be called a "Super patience board" because you need a lot of patience to use it. Here's how it worked: it would take two people, otherwise the process is much slower. One would say the letter of the alphabet and the other would watch for an intentional double blink from Michael's beautiful blue but pain-filled eyes. If Michael blinked twice, it was yes to the letter. As you can imagine, we were spelling out letter by letter his entire response. And this was no fucking Wheel of Fortune game, no this was a test of patience from everyone involved. We learned to streamline it by guessing his words, or saying – is it a vowel? Two blinks meant yes, and one blink was a no. And Michael would also just shake his head yes or no, even though he wasn't supposed to for the sake of his neck.

This was such a sad process. Along with everything else Michael lost, he had lost his voice too. And this was intense because Michael's first love language is words, he's a talker, and he loves to communicate and tell elaborate stories and his curiosity and passion for others comes through strong. It's one of the traits that really drew me to him in the first place. For him to be limited and not be able to talk was simply awful, grueling, and spoon-fed all of us more grief.

The first thing post-surgery he spelled out for me was this, "Stop touching my head."

My stomach dropped and I felt my breath struggle. Since I didn't know what sensations he was still able to feel in his body, I made the assumption he could feel his head and forehead, thus I touched him there often.

This was hard to hear. I thought it was going to be some grand thank you...and turns out I was bothering him. Touch is my primary love language – it is how I show my love and appreciation. Hearing his response was bittersweet; on the one hand, I was happy he could say this and yet I felt bad because I unknowingly had been annoying him. This was the last thing I wanted to do; I only wanted him to feel comfortable because he was very uncomfortable. We were all uncomfortable, and looking back I see now I was just trying to soothe my nervous system.

After this, I stopped touching him as much as I had been. I even became afraid to touch him because his system was compromised. Michael was also having a condition with paralysis where your nerves feel like they're on fire; any touch exacerbates this condition. I wanted to get into the medical hospital bed and just hold him, but I was afraid to with all the tubes connecting him to the ventilator, his drip feed to his meds, and his feeding tube. With much less touch, the result for me was that *Grief* got more comfortable in her campsite she was setting up within me.

While she was getting comfortable, we were all uncomfortable and navigating a mountain of things – the medical issues, the complications, along with dealing with grief and loss, many losses – loss of touch, loss of his voice, he even lost his laugh which is different to this day. We can't even remember what it sounded like and just thinking about this brings up more grief.

Later he spelled out for me, "The accident got me to this point, now I have to figure out why I am here. I need to know what to do to heal. I am going inward to figure it out."

He then closed his eyes and when he opened them again to look at me, I said, "I trust you." And he then mouthed thank you. I trusted him, and I trusted him to figure it out. And the one thing I know for sure regardless of all the trauma drama, and the PhD study of the body, and the sense of helplessness and the fear of the unknown, the future...the one thing I know for sure is I love this man. I love you, Michael Mathieu! My love for him was crystal clear, like a beacon of light, or a sword of truth.

Going within to figure it out seemed right; he was in the *cocoon goo* stage of metamorphosis from being an able-bodied human to a being with paralysis. He was deep in the depths of exploration; he was in serious adjustment mode. He was dying into a new way of being. I refer to it as *cocoon goo* because a caterpillar wraps itself in a cocoon and then its entire being dissolves into this mysterious goo and is thrust into an uncomfortable transformation stage of becoming a being with wings. I imagined this often in these early days, trusting this process to eventually bring us wings. His cocoon was my deep sense of love for him along with the love of his family and our dear community. We made a cocoon of love for him to simply go within and do his healing.

In those first few post-surgery days it was as if he was running an inner marathon as he was relearning how to exist again. He had to learn how to breathe all over again. It was like he was a newborn. He relied on a ventilator, eventually his day would have scheduled times to be without the machine, and each day a bit more time. He was doing really well, and we were filled with hope as each day he would be able to breathe better on his own. He was also able to talk to us when he was off the vent. Then salmon entered the picture.

CHAPTER 5

SALMON
TOOK HIS BREATH AWAY

"Tame wild disappointment
With caress unmoved and cold
Make of it a parka
For your soul."

—Alice Walker

It was seven days post-surgery, September 4th, and our friend Annie fed him salmon. And at the time, Michael was thrilled to eat because he hadn't had any real food since August 27th. He'd been on a feeding tube. The nurses and staff thought he would be fine to eat as well. But they were all very wrong.

Early the next day or rather, in the middle of the night he called for us to come. His dad, Armand, woke me at 3:46 a.m. knocking on my door, "Beth, get up, Michael called me and asked us to all come to the hospital!"

I jumped out of bed and got dressed without hesitation. I was *on* instantly. Remember *Shock*? She sleeps in her clothes in case she needs to jump into action; she's always ready to go. If he's calling for us now, it means something serious happened and he needs us there. We weren't told what was happening. His sister Linda came with me in my car. I drove as fast as I could, I ignored the red traffic lights; drove right through them after making sure no one was coming, of course. Red lights make no sense when it is 4:00 a.m. and most of the world is deep in sleep and your loved one has urged you to come to see them at the hospital. *Shock* was driving and she was determined to get there as fast as she could.

We arrived at 4:15 a.m. He had had a respiratory arrest and almost died...again. He called for us to come because he was in a panic and thought he was going to die, and he didn't want to die alone. His mama bear of a nurse, Rhonda, was in the room when his eyes rolled back, and he disappeared. Thank God she was there because she jumped into action to save him. He had coded blue. Why is it known as code blue? Because you actually have blue-looking skin? Okay, I had to ask Google – code blue simply means a cardiac or respiratory arrest. It should be called code puke greenish-grey because this was the color he turned.

Later that afternoon Michael coded blue again. Greg, Michael's brother-in-law came bursting through the ICU door to the waiting area and yelled to me in a panicked voice, high-pitched and strained, "Beth! Come now – Michael's having a seizure!"

I had just come in from a much-needed walk around the neighborhood, (which is probably why I stopped going for walks when at the hospital). I bolted through the ICU door and ran as fast as I could to be with him. There were men in suits by the door holding yellow plastic briefcases, and more and more hospital staff piling in for some color of code that was broadcast on the speakers throughout the hospital. All kinds of people came rushing into the tiny room – the social worker, more nurses, and security guards suddenly appeared to guard the door. It was like a hospital business meeting, and I thought to myself – is this what happens when someone is about to die – all these official strangers come piling in to see the action? Michael's dad plowed straight through the security guards while saying in a stern strong voice, "I need to be with my wife!"

He rushed over to stand next to Bonnie who was huddled next to me. Then what happened next is etched in my memory: Michael's skin turned an awful gray-greenish color, and his eyes were rolling back in his head. Amy, his nurse, started yelling at him while touching his shoulders, "Michael, where are you going? Come back here!! Michael! Michael!"

I felt paralyzed standing in shock watching this happen and was just saying over and over out loud in a steady pace like a metronome, "Oh my God, oh my God, oh my God."

Meanwhile, I was vigilantly watching our friend Rohini's face who had been there visiting him. My eyes were darting back and forth from hers to Michael's in what was probably only 30 seconds but felt like a lifetime. Rohini is a doctor and if she went into full-on panic, then I would too. Even back then I had logical self-care in some sort of twisted upside-down way.

Michael did come back to us. The color of his skin returned quickly, and he actually looked right at me when his eyes were back to normal, and he winked at me! I thought to myself and wondered – who did you just see and what did they just tell you?

I was relieved, yet not, as I was seriously concerned about what had just happened. Michael doesn't remember this moment at all. I never did learn who he talked to or what he saw on the other side. What I did know is he had almost died again. He had had a respiratory arrest, he never lost his pulse, but he stopped breathing.

Later they did a fancy brain scan for many long hours to conclude he was not seizing, and his brain was not damaged. I could have told them that with the way he had been making demands and asking many specific health questions through the superboard communication system once again that his brain was fine and functioning. I was grateful Michael always wore his helmet while biking. It's a reminder for you and your loved ones to always wear one as well. We didn't have to deal with him also having a TBI (traumatic brain injury). I was very relieved and thankful for this.

After this long weird, awful day, I started sleeping with my phone on. I never used to in order to shut out the electromagnetic frequencies (EMFs) while sleeping. The phone went weird though, and I thought the battery was not working, it was as if it was connected to Michael. It would stop and restart in the middle of the night; like it was trying to rewire itself. I tried getting a new battery and it kept doing the same thing. If only we could have gotten Michael something as simple as a new battery and just replace his blown-apart bits.

Yes, if only we could have replaced the parts that were majorly impacted by the accident – mainly his spinal cord and cervical vertebrae. Actually, anything having to do with his throat or neck was an issue. The human body is a complex and extraordinary system with interconnections in order for it to work well. I was suddenly thrust into an unofficial PhD study about how the spinal cord works, as well as how *Grief* and *Trauma* set up camp in the body.

I am not sure if feeding him salmon triggered the respiratory arrest, but we did learn anything having to do with swallowing and eating would be compromised. The next day he was scheduled for more surgery – to have a tracheostomy and a PEG tube (a feeding tube) because he would no longer be able to eat normally. I also lost my appetite, yet I would force myself to eat. I remember looking at my plate of food and feeling exhausted when I knew I had to put it in my mouth and chew and swallow. I did it because I knew I needed it to keep going on this marathon path.

What's a tracheostomy? It's a process to insert a tube in your trachea to assist breathing because the airway is obstructed. It is inserted at the bottom of your throat, or about two inches below the Adam's apple. If you see Michael today, you will see a scar there which is where this tube was for a few weeks. This was connected to the ventilator tubes which essentially became his lungs. He was having serious issues with breathing; a thing I took for granted before all this. The simple act of breathing, when you break your neck at C4 and C5, breathing is no longer a simple process. In fact, Michael remembers being up on the trail after his accident and his breathing became more of a struggle, he had to will it to happen. He felt as if he was on his last breath when the rescue crews showed up. Where's your breath right now reader? Take a moment to notice its flow and just simply breathe for a few moments...

Michael had to learn how to breathe. And it was bittersweet to watch him relearn how to do many simple daily living tasks – breathing, eating, swallowing, talking. And the reason you have an audible voice is that air comes in and goes over the vocal cords, and a trach tube bypasses this. As a result, he lost his voice again and couldn't speak to us. He lost his voice while I found mine – I began to speak up with fierce honesty and started dropping the f-bomb all over the place.

And one thing I was fucking clear about was my decision to stay with him. After surgery, Michael had asked me three times to leave him. After his third request, I told him once and for all to stop asking me to leave. If he stayed and chose this life, I would too. I never even questioned it.

CHAPTER 6

FAWNING AND GRIEF

"When others tell you to get over your grief,
you can tell them to get over their need for you to get over your grief."

—Joanne Cacchiatore

Many others questioned it; wondering why I didn't leave him. After the accident, many people asked me – how long were you two dating? As if there was a magic number for my mad decision to stay. Love doesn't need a number, but I get their logic. The accident happened three years after we started dating. We had just taken the big step of moving in together and our relationship felt solid. This was blown wide open when we were catapulted into a strange reality most couples never have to navigate – me sitting in the ER in the middle of the night with Michael on a gurney prepped for intense and complicated surgery.

Why did I stay? I couldn't imagine bailing on the life partner I'd waited on for many years simply because his neck was broken. If anything, the accident actually bonded us even closer together as I tuned in and got the ball rolling on his rescue down from the trail. I did ask myself often—how are we going to live like this, or what's it going to be like? I knew it would be hard, and I also knew I'd have to simply live my way into the answer.

Living into the answer was bizarre. I was dealing with how others responded to all this or didn't as they just couldn't deal with it at all. My life was consumed with navigating the trauma drama in the hospital and learning to suddenly be living with my in-laws. Linda and Greg ended up staying for about six months, and his parents stayed for the first month and then would return a few months later for another few weeks. I was also in a sudden unexpected apprenticeship to grief; I'd been swallowed and was deep in the bowels of grief itself. I was experiencing grief as an inside job.

Grief joined me sitting around the fire along with *Shock* and *Trauma*. They stayed by my side, while those who were close to me ran away as if accidents and disability were contagious, airborne diseases. Actually, this happened to me. My best friend Tauna shared that another friend of ours told her she didn't want to come to visit us because she believed her husband might get in some kind of tragic biking accident if she did!

I became what people try to avoid in this Western culture. Eventually, we all succumb to illness and death. Shit happens and grief arrives. People don't like to be around grievers and they shy away from illness, loss, and death. It's a reminder that we truly aren't in control of anything, and accidents do indeed happen. It's as if I was walking around with a flashing fluorescent sign above me with an obnoxious buzzing sound. Its message was this, "You too will lose it all! You too will lose your abilities, and we're all going to die someday!"

And if we're blessed, most of us will gracefully make it to old age and others may not. Some will watch their abilities dwindle and fall off slowly and there will be those who will be catapulted into old age like Michael was. His actual fall was small in distance, but the lasting impact was huge. He went from being in the prime of his life to being an infant and an elder at the same time. He went from being 48 to 98 as he needed help with every mundane and important physical task like shitting, peeing, picking his nose, and eating. Yes, picking your nose is an important task and it's something I no longer take for granted! So now I proudly pick my nose and I revel in the sheer pleasure of it.

I felt like I'd been thrust into elderhood from an emotional and spiritual standpoint. I wanted to ask for the senior discount. Seniority doesn't just come from age; it also comes from life experience. I'd been initiated into deep soul loss, which unfortunately isn't recognized by AARP.

I was being initiated by grief and I wish someone had prepared me better for it. Even my clinical studies in graduate school failed me. I did my internship at a hospice, and I wrote my thesis on the use of the mandala in art therapy for grief. But hardly any of it was supportive and no amount of reading from Kubler-Ross or Worden and all the others helped me when I was living it.

Living it absolutely sucks...sudden loss is hard. Not only does it shatter your life, it also rearranges your address book. You actually have more than one loss. It's so very complicated and complex. Grief is cruel in this way, because not only are you dealing with the initial loss, but then you have other losses because of that loss, also known as "secondary losses."

And it didn't just affect me and Michael, the shock and grief rippled out into our community, and everyone was impacted in some way. As I started to run into people, I was beginning to see how it impacted them, or not. I was beginning to have such bitter and sometimes sweet interactions. The friends I thought for sure would be there for me weren't and people we didn't know well came in closer. It didn't make any sense. Many of my friends were frightened away. And even when they would come closer in, they would say and do stupid things and then I'd go away. Our community looked like the inside of Michael's neck; C5 was completely shattered and gone and our community core was obliterated. They had to create a cage to rebuild Michael's neck, just like we had to rebuild our community.

A week after the accident I went to the Sunday morning Contact Improv Lab, and immediately all eyes were on me. I had twenty people swarm towards me like a moth to a flame. They wanted to all hug me at once; they simply surrounded me with a big group hug. After this group embrace, I was given hug after hug. It was a lot to take in, but at the time I welcomed it all. The squeezing, solid embraces infused me with the strength to keep going. And each time I went to Sunday Lab in those first few months, I'd be inundated with attention and questions. Eventually, I wanted to wear a t-shirt that said, "Please treat me like the Beth before the accident."

I started to feel like a celebrity. There were times I wanted to remain anonymous and just sneak in quietly like I used to. I didn't want to be the famous person whose partner was stripped of all his physical abilities. I didn't want to be the sidekick to this tragedy, yet I was.

Eventually, to avoid these interactions when I was in public, I started to wear hats, hoodies, and sunglasses. Or I'd just go the other direction to avoid someone I knew. Sometimes a quick trip to the store to get coffee beans, bacon and bananas ended up in an unofficial therapy session in the middle of the grocery aisle, and shopping would take a lot longer than expected.

I attended another Contact Improv dance event a few weeks after my group hug experience. I arrived at the small space where the wall of windows fogged up because of the sweaty bodies doing serious dancing inside. One of my friends saw me walking to the door and came running out to greet me. She immediately bombarded me with a very strong embrace and together we collapsed to the concrete sidewalk in a puddle of tears. Then something odd happened. As she was holding and supporting me, it switched and suddenly I was the stronger one holding her. I tried to let go and she kept holding on to me, I just held her immense grief instead of her holding mine. I felt puzzled and confused yet strong at the same time, which didn't make any sense.

Another time after Contact Improv Lab, we were packed into the coat room putting on clothes, coats, and shoes. There would be pockets of people catching up and we'd often bump into each other on our way out the door. It was as if the dancing continued since we had just been rolling around on each other.

One man dressed in 80's parachute pants with funky colors and patterns on them looked up at me as I was inching by him. His glance caught mine. I nodded and said hello. He then asked me, "How's Michael?"

I sighed inside and was grateful yet annoyed because the day before I had just spent an hour crafting an update on the Lotsa Helping Hands website answering this very question. I took a deep breath and replied calmly, "Did you see the Lotsa site update yesterday?

Obviously, he didn't, otherwise, he wouldn't have asked. He replied, "No. I'm not on there."

And I said firmly, "Well if you really want to know how he's doing and stay updated, the website is the best way, I can't keep having these conversations every time I go out. Please check it out."

And I walked away, and I didn't even feel bad. I began to be rude as a way to self-preserve. I had to learn how to be forthright yet polite. Yet why couldn't I just be a mess when I had to answer that simple question for the 1000th time? It was a beautiful conundrum though – to have so many people asking about Michael.

Surprisingly, people hardly asked how I was doing. I had a small number of dear friends who would take the time to just ask me. I am grateful for them. You know who you are. I say a heartfelt thanks to those who knew I was also laying on the hospital bed undergoing my own kind of transformation as I was learning how to be the partner of someone with a spinal cord injury.

I no longer fit in my old life and thus my interactions with my friends, acquaintances, and colleagues became very awkward. I was thrust out of my old life when Michael was thrown from his mountain bike. During this first year, I was in a peer supervision group with mostly friends who were therapists. Attending this group used to be such a highlight of my professional life, but it started to feel uncomfortable. I showed up one day and a friend I didn't know well asked me eagerly, "How's Michael?"

I paused to figure out how to answer. My friend Jenny leaned in closer with curiosity and the one who asked the question looked at me with eyes filled with pity. I said, "Well, he's had some digestive issues lately and he's really struggling."

Jenny asked me more questions and before I knew it, we went down the rabbit hole of parasites and digestive health. After a few minutes, our conversation came to an end, and my friend who originally asked the question said, "Well, I didn't need to know all that."

The other therapists were arriving at this time, so our conversation came to an abrupt end. I felt unfinished and uneasy as if knots were tightening inside me. I realized later I was quite angry at her for the short and frankly rude response like it was her inside thoughts leaking out. I wished I would have said, "If you didn't need to hear this, then why the fuck did you ask me? Just to be polite?"

This is when I started thinking it'd be great to give a multiple-choice question in response to theirs. I'll give you an answer based on these categories:

a. How much time do you have?

b. Do you want the superficial answer?

c. How much do you really want to know?

Basically, I wanted people not to ask if they didn't have time to hear the answer or hear the truth, which was often hard and complicated. And what surprised me the most was she was a really good therapist. And maybe this was why she didn't want to know – hell, we listen and hold healing space for others all day long. I felt dropped by her and angered by her response. I started being hesitant with my responses after this. I started fawning, not knowing it was even a thing at the time.

Fawning is a nervous system response where we people-please to fit in and belong; we override our natural responses. It's a social or physical response that overrides your truth to appease others. You take care of them instead of honoring your own emotional experience. And we do this to remain part of a group. It's based on not wanting to be ostracized. Fawning happens often in grief because there is such a stigma around grief anyway, and we'll do anything to belong. Grief is taboo and shame comes along with it in this culture where we don't know how to grieve very well.

I had been fawning a lot and it went on for the first few years. On Winter Solstice 2013, I attended a one-day yoga retreat put on by a friend I'd known for many years in our Contact Improv dance community. We weren't close. But right before the accident, we had just started to hang out more to deepen our connection.

I was apprehensive about going; I wondered if I'd be able to remain anonymous. I wanted to just be there and tend to my body and mind which were still dealing with the trauma of it all. I nervously walked through the door of the yoga studio which was tucked away near my neighborhood in the back of an old warehouse. It was a mirror for my life in some ways – such beauty and healing taking place inside an old, dilapidated warehouse.

My mind was churning – would I know anyone else? Would I have to explain my story? Would I be bombarded with questions about how Michael was doing? Would I be barraged with all those well-intentioned questions which would miss me? The focus was mostly on the one who was injured and not on the caregiver. The caregiver gets stuck on the sidelines, like a middle schooler at an awkward dance waiting to be noticed.

And then it happened, at some point in this yoga workshop, my friend shared with the entire group of twelve women the story of my partner crashing his mountain bike and breaking his neck. Yes, here in this healing space the story was brought up. And each time in the beginning when I was asked this, I learned I could cut off my emotions, go on autopilot and tell it without feeling anything at all. I became quite an expert at it. Without knowing it, she put me on the spot and asked me in front of eager eyes, ears, and hearts, "Beth, how are you doing with all of this?"

I felt like a deer in the headlights. I was still in the trauma phase, and I didn't want to be the center of attention. I was just a normal human being undergoing very abnormal circumstances. And I didn't want to preach about what I was doing to cope. I know now her question came from a place of well-intentioned curiosity and her sense of helplessness. And in fact, most platitudes come from this place; humans will do just about anything to avoid feeling out of control or weak and unable to fix the problem.

The women leaned in closer from their separated spaces delineated by their precious yoga mats. They were drawn towards me as if I were some kind of magnet. And they truly wanted to know how I was doing this, and to be honest, I did too. My life had become a bad car accident scene on the highway where all the onlookers just have to slow down, craning their necks to see. My life was one large wreck and people came in closer to see it. Well, this was not completely true – people were either scared away or wanted to come in for more. They only wanted to see it, get off from it, but not stay in it with me. Only a very selective few stayed.

Suddenly I put an invisible border around my yoga mat as my heart dropped. I felt all at once a barrage of emotions – I was stunned, surprised, disappointed, sad, and frustrated. I was angry but wouldn't realize it until later. I was fawning again without even knowing I was doing it. I was also tender and curious about these women anxiously staring at me, some had tears welling up as they probably put themselves in my shoes and imagined losing their own partners to quadriplegia.

Part of me wanted to tell my friend to fuck off for not giving me a heads-up that I was going to be a featured part of the workshop. I wanted to grab my yoga mat and run out the door. I no longer felt safe and suddenly felt like the other, the famous one. And then I began to receive the pity looks and the pity hugs, which would land on me like green slime. Yet it wasn't all bad. It was a bizarre experience. A part of me craved the attention, yet I also wanted to spit it out like it was rotten food.

In this moment, my emotions were churning, and my mind was confused. I honestly didn't know how to answer her simple question. I sat wordlessly for a bit and then I simply said, "I'm just doing what I have to do."

I was a living example of one of my favorite lines in the poem by Oriah Mountain Dreamer called *The Invitation*. In it, she writes, "I want to know if you can get up after the night of grief and despair, weary and bruised to the bone, and do what needs to be done to feed the children."

This was the best explanation of how I was doing what I was doing, I was simply doing what I had to do. I felt like my answer disappointed them, and they expected some mind-blowing mic-drop advice on how to carry on in the face of adversity. But when you're in it, you're just doing what you have to do each moment, each hour of each difficult day.

Later I realized I felt incredibly angry because she took away my anonymity. She didn't ask for consent to speak freely about my emotional process. I had become "inspiration porn." I learned this term in an article by Shane Clifton[2] who also had a tragic accident and was the same level quadriplegic as Michael, C5.

I wish people would be more mindful when asking someone who's going through a traumatic loss. I'd like people to ask this, "Is it okay if I ask you about it? Or would you rather I just be here with you?"

And I wish they'd be prepared for a response that is hard to hear. We need to be better about being with someone else's pain and discomfort. I once ran into an acquaintance at Target. We were in the middle of the main aisle in between the sappy cards and shampoos. She was there with her two toddlers. This was about a year after when we'd already been living back in Boulder for a bit (which is a long story coming in the next few chapters). She said hello and then asked me, "Well now that you're back in Boulder are more people in the community coming around?"

---

[2] Article from the Christian Century, March 27, 2019, called "The Good and Dependent Life." He also wrote a book called "Crippled Grace: Disability, Virtue Ethics and the Good Life."

And my answer surprised her, and I didn't sugar coat it either, I simply said, without hesitation, "No, no they're not."

And then we both stood there awkwardly near the cards and shampoos. She didn't know what to say and neither did I. Where was the shampoo to clean out my community in these situations? Or at least a sappy card to make it all okay for a moment. I either wanted a greeting card to bypass it or a lot of shampoo to clean it up, and I'm pretty sure she did too.

And this is why we fawn because I believe I lost her as a community member at this uncomfortable moment. If I had given her the response she was hoping to hear versus the utter truth, well, maybe we'd still be connected to this day.

I wish people would think about receiving ALL the answers before they ask these simple questions. I refused to say our life was okay when it wasn't. I wouldn't bypass the ugliness with false nice comments. But people just wanted to hear we were okay. I really just needed people who weren't scared to be in the shitshow of our life. I needed people to walk with me in the muck of our lives and stay with me in the discomfort of it all.

Being the unofficial featured guest happened so many times, I should have started charging people for it. In the spring of 2014, I went to a yoga retreat at a beautiful resort near Sayulita, Mexico called Haramara. My dear friend Rainey was hosting it. She's a yoga instructor, embodied healer, and Somatic Experiencing practitioner. She has the most amazing curly hair-tight ringlets framing her beautiful face and she has a deep soothing voice too.

Rainey and I instantly became friends a few years prior when Michael and I visited her and her husband in Seattle for Thanksgiving. Her husband's name is also Michael and is a dear friend of my Michael. The Michaels immediately bonded when they met at a visceral manipulation training in 2008. I loved watching them geek out together about how the body worked, which they'd do often. And I loved receiving bodywork from each of them, they'd both give us sessions and then compare what they found.

Rainey and Michael invited me on the yoga trip because they knew I needed to be on the land near the ocean and just listen to jungle sounds, eat freshly cooked fish, hear the ocean waves, sleep deeply in an outdoor palapa, tend to my body, and feel the sun on my skin. It was a most welcomed and needed trip.

One day I laid down on the beach where water met earth. I sank into the soft wet sand with gravity, being generous with my weight. I closed my eyes and waited until the waves came and pushed me around. It was ironic as it was how Michael would have to be if he could have been there; his body unable to move. I'd be taken by surprise when a stronger wave would knock me around and I laughed with delight like I was a five-year-old. I was mesmerized by this experience, and I played with the water and sand for about an hour. I was like a rock tossed in and out of the ocean, with each wave shaking out and smoothing the trauma within me like how water creates pearls over time or smooths river rocks.

On the first evening, we gathered for dinner as a large group, all sitting around the large table in the main outdoor dining hall covered with a roof made from thatched palm tree branches. The ocean breeze was coming in and the sun was about to set on the expansive horizon before us. There was an orange-tinged glow all around. We were eating totopos, the Mexican version of chips served with fresh salsa. If you know me, you know I love eating chips and so I was thoroughly enjoying myself and reveling in the normality of it all.

As we were waiting for our dinners, we were doing the usual chit-chat to get to know each other since we'd be together for the next six days. We were asking things like where we're from and what we do. Then I learned my story can drop like a bomb and redirect the entire conversation down a dark rabbit hole; my life interruption can be the biggest conversation changer. I was in the middle of delivering a chip into my mouth when I was bombarded with a landfall of questions: how did the accident happen, were you with him? Does he have any ability to move? Can he talk? Does he also have a TBI? Was he wearing a helmet? How long had you been dating him?

The chip in my mouth now tasted like cardboard and I went through the motions of chewing and swallowing, but I was no longer tasting the pleasure of it as I was trying to find the words to answer all their questions. I wish I would have just kept eating all the chips instead of saying those simple words, "I'm here to heal from my partner becoming a quadriplegic because he broke his neck."

See, did it just take your appetite away too?

I was continuing to learn I had to be careful about what I say, how to say it, and when to say it. To care for myself, I had to be careful with others. It's really fucked up, I had to set aside my grief so I could take care of another's discomfort. Again, I had to fawn. I was continuing to learn I could choose to remain anonymous for the sake of my healing. If I disclosed this huge and shocking part of my reality, then I'd have to possibly take care of the listener.

It became part of my routine before meeting someone or going to a gathering, I'd check in with myself – do I want to disclose my traumatic story or remain anonymous? My answer depended on how resourced I felt. It also depended on the relationship with the person or group. And the whole dynamic would change if I did know someone who already knew my story.

This is when I started to live small to save myself. I began to share very little which was unlike me. I usually share much more than I ought to, as I love to share about my life and it's also really hard to lie as I wear my heart on my sleeve. I went to a few gatherings after this where I never let out our story and was relieved to see I didn't know anyone. I reveled in being normal, yet it felt odd because I had a huge, awful secret within me.

I had many weird experiences going out in the world when Michael no longer could because he was in the hospital. Just going out to a restaurant felt odd, seeing all the able-bodied people easily moving around, feeding themselves, and having a good time was upsetting for me.

I attended my goddaughter Hannah's bat mitzvah in May of 2015. Hannah is the daughter of my dear friend Linda who I called to be with me in the ER on the first night.

I was sitting at the table covered with a white tablecloth and enjoying a glass of red wine with my tiny plate of appetizers. I've never understood tiny plates. I love to eat, and I appreciate food. I met the eyes of an acquaintance, and she came towards me and said those dreaded but beautiful words, "How's Michael doing?"

I paused. I noticed my heart sank. And I began to feel myself pulling away from the celebration. And instead of going on autopilot, I simply replied while looking directly into her eyes, "Thanks for asking, I appreciate it and right now what I really want to do is to celebrate Hannah, I don't want to go into the details, but he's mostly fine."

I felt so proud of myself, I prioritized me not her, and didn't even feel guilty for saying this. I had finally become a woman with discernment and boundaries, and I began to use them often. This accident gifted me fierce honesty and I wasn't afraid to use it. I was learning when people asked me how Michael was doing, it could put me straight back into the center of the storm. Whatever I was doing or trying to do would be washed away and it might take me a while to center myself again. I began to manage my response to grief and deliberately compartmentalize it. Slowing down and checking in with myself helped about whether I wanted to open the wound in the moment.

I also had total strangers giving me unsolicited advice after the accident, even a few years after. In February of 2015, I remember distinctly wanting to punch one woman in the gut when I was introduced to her at a Soul Collage workshop which was hosted by my dear friend Raven.

I love how Raven and I met – our fingertips collided on the dance floor at our ecstatic dance community in Denver back in 2008 and we've been dancing in a strong friendship ever since. Raven is a powerful woman, she works in the corporate world, yet she also practices the creative healing arts through her art, creativity, and nature-based rituals and ceremonies. She is a modern shamanic healer and is a juxtaposition – dealing with her career while also being a force of nature with her creative soul practices.

For some reason, Raven had mentioned to this woman what had happened to Michael. Upon meeting me she went on and on about how I didn't need to stay with Michael because he's a quadriplegic and I could choose a different life. I was quite aghast – as if I didn't know this! Because of this, she was immediately placed in the – 'get the fuck out of my community' category. I did not befriend this woman, and at the time I remember thinking in my head, "What the hell? Is this really what you say to someone who's dealing with living a life full of transition as her partner's still learning how to be in the body which no longer works the way it had for 48 years? I mean, really!"

I was still in a state of trauma and was keenly aware of platitudes. People offered kind words which only seemed to soothe themselves, whereas, what I needed was for them to simply stand in the middle of the chaos with me. I felt disconnected and cut off immediately from her and pissed as hell. And then I had to be with her in the workshop for the next five hours. I just dove into my creative bubble and put my guard up. Art doesn't ask you those kinds of questions or tell you to leave your partner. It provides a place to make sense of all of it. Little did I know then I would be navigating many awkward moments like this.

Her comment was super unsupportive. Many comments were unhelpful around this time, yet all well-intentioned. What I know now is it would have been better simply to acknowledge how hard it must have been, and I must love him a lot to stay. Yeah, this would have felt much better, and I would have let her in. I just needed acknowledgment and companionship. It's simple really, but when your community was also caught up in the trauma, many people couldn't handle just hanging out in the discomfort of our new life. I developed a keen radar for truth; I had no tolerance for bullshit. Come at me with a vulnerable and open heart, you're in; come at me with pity and platitudes, the walls go up.

The unsolicited advice and pity landed on me like yellow mucus, I wanted to simply wipe it off and leave it behind...but I didn't, those comments really pissed me off inside. And in a way, I wonder if it's what kept molding me into who I am today. It gave me something to push against to allow me to come into who I was becoming. Just like a baby pushing against mom's abdominal walls to be born, I too was birthing myself into a new way of being.

While Michael was fighting for his life in the ICU and then later learning how to be in the newborn body of a 48-year-old quadriplegic, I too was learning how to be in this reality I didn't want to be my life.

CHAPTER 7

ROCKS OF MY TRANSFORMATION

"I am not a victim of my life. What I went through pulled a warrior out of me and it is my greatest honor to be her."

—Rupi Kaur

But this was my life, and I intentionally chose it, or rather, it chose me. And I want to clarify, it was never an option to leave. At some point early on I realized my life felt like a marathon, not that I'd ever run one or ever planned to. I just knew to keep going, I'd have to change many things if I wanted to stay in it for the long haul. I would need breaks and some serious kind of neon green or yellow-colored electrolyte sports drink[3], which I never drink. I'd also need a team to help me along the way. I would need to have what I called radical self-care. And I'd have to

---

[3] We make our own electrolyte drink without all the sugar and food coloring. Here's a simple recipe: adjust as needed for your body. For one liter of water add 1/4 teaspoon sea salt, 1/4 teaspoon potassium citrate, and 1/8-1/4 teaspoon of liquid magnesium. If you need to sweeten it, add stevia.

find non-traditional and out-of-the-box ways to support the enormity of my situation for my survival.

I started sleeping with rocks. I have always had a love and affinity for rocks, rooted in my relationship with my paternal grandma Ruth who had an extensive rock collection. Every time she traveled she gathered a few rocks to bring home with her. The garden under her carport was full of clusters of her traveling rock companions. Each collection was marked with a plastic margarine top attached to a popsicle stick that was stuck in the ground. In her beautiful cursive handwriting, she wrote where they came from – Utah, Montana, Colorado, Sweden, Norway, France, Spain, and so on.

It gives me both grief and love remembering these rocks and I wonder if they're still laying there in the driveway. She died when I was nineteen of glioblastoma, one of the worst kinds of brain cancer. I wasn't a part of the cleaning crew when they moved everything out of the house on Pasternack Place in San Diego. But if I could go back, I'd love to help just to see what other collections she had, and I'd take a few of those rocks and their labels with me.

Since my grandma Ruth gifted me her love of rocks, it made sense I reached for them to help me deal with our situation. A few days after the accident I was still feeling as if the inside of me was shaking with small aftershocks. I found an oval-shaped rock about six inches long and three inches wide in the hospital parking lot. I took it home and started sleeping with it. When I grabbed it, I didn't know why, and I certainly didn't know how I'd be using it. I needed something from the place where he was, and Longmont United Hospital was surrounded by smooth river rocks. Ironic because Michael was lying in an ICU bed after hitting one large slab of rock on the trail.

At bedtime, I placed the rock on my heart area near the sternum, the bone in the middle of the upper chest. The weight of the rock reminded my body to settle and to feel the support of the ground below me through gravity. I placed it on my upper chest for the first few nights, then it traveled down my body over the next few weeks. First, I placed it on one side of my lungs or the rib cage, then the other, then on one side of my pelvis, then the other. After a few nights of this, the shaking subsided. But I kept it in my bed anyway, even if I didn't use it on my body. I placed it where Michael should have been. Sleeping with the rock was better than sleeping with the huge gap his absence created.

For the first few weeks, I'd wake up and have a split-second moment of sweet amnesia and then I'd reach for his side of the bed and be met with the cold reality of my life from the rock. I'd cry as all the details of my new life would come rushing into my consciousness. This was my routine for the first few weeks; moving from this sweet, liminal forgetful space into the remembering, and then I'd begin my day sobbing.

After crying, part of me was ready to get up and do what needed to be done. I was relentless about getting to the hospital as soon as I could to support him and see how he was doing. I started wearing his gray T-shirt I had given him a year before, on it were these words written in bold bright orange letters – RELENTLESSLY AWESOME.

I felt both full of grief and relentlessly awesome to be able to be with this situation. It felt odd to feel both at the same time. And in some ways, it couldn't have happened to two better people ready to do this work – being a psychotherapist, I had studied and worked with grief already and Michael being an amazing osteopathic bodyworker, was super knowledgeable and curious about how the body worked. I handled the emotions, and he handled the body. There were times I thought he knew more about the body than his nurses and doctors did. He was a body geek and I started becoming one too. It was as if I took a sideways sabbatical to learn how the body keeps living with a spinal cord injury and how grief and trauma affect the body, mind, and spirit as well.

I learned a lot about the vagus nerve, which is responsible for the rest and digest part of the nervous system known as parasympathetic. The vagus nerve doesn't run through the spinal cord, instead it "wanders" from the cranium, down through the face and neck, into the torso to attach to all the vital organs, and ends at the anus and sphincter muscles. In case you're wondering why it feels really good to take a big dump – now you know why! This wandering nerve keeps the organs working so we can do other things besides reminding ourselves to breathe in and out, digest our food, and keep our hearts beating. This amazing wandering nerve was responsible for keeping Michael alive because thankfully it wasn't impacted by the accident like his spinal cord was.

The vagus nerve is the closest to the skin's surface in the area of the sternum. Without knowing this at the time, I intuitively placed the rock where the vagus nerve was the most accessible to touch. Or perhaps it was my grandma Ruth guiding me to do this. Placing the rock there helped settle my nervous system which was continuing to recalibrate itself just like Michael was adjusting to his new body, I too was getting to know mine as well.

Everything was a mess – my body was a mess from the overload of cortisol. My nervous system was overactive due to all the stress. I was also having sleep issues which didn't help. One day a small envelope appeared anonymously on my porch, inside were a few Ambien pills with a handwritten note saying these would help me sleep. I told Rohini, our doctor friend, that someone had gifted these little pills to me but I was hesitant to take them. She looked me straight in the eyes and sternly told me to use any means necessary to sleep. I surrendered and received this most needed pharmaceutical intervention.

My physical world was a mirror of my life at the time. Being there for Michael was the priority, not keeping my house clean and organized. I didn't have time to tend to things like I used to. My room was in a state of chaos, I wasn't watering the plants, and my clothes were in various states of piles – clean and needing to be put away, to be worn again, or dirty. (But at least I had these piles!)

My mouth was dirty – I started cussing A LOT. I must have said the "f" word more times than I could count and still do daily. I told my parents to just get used to my new potty mouth. Like most kids, we weren't allowed to cuss, and it was still frowned upon, but I just couldn't stop cussing and it felt like it was actually helping me to cope with the fucking situation.

My relationships were falling apart. I was aware I couldn't be there for my closest friends, and I felt immense guilt for this, yet I also knew I didn't have the capacity. What happens to friendships when one person is in a state of overwhelm such as this? The reciprocal (ness) of friendship just doesn't work anymore. It was out of balance, and I was worried I might lose some of my dearest friends. But really, is any friendship ever truly balanced? I suppose it is if you're both in a stable place emotionally, mentally, physically, and spiritually. This is a tall order, right? Where did we get this idea our relationships have to be balanced?

The friendship I was worried about the most equally surprised me – it was with my best friend Tauna. I didn't think the ones in my innermost circle would be afraid to stay around. Tauna was the one who rallied in the beginning and set up our Lotsa Healing Hands website and wrote some posts to the community because I just couldn't. A few months after the accident I noticed she wasn't calling as often, nor was she leaving me messages anymore. Her sudden absence felt like I went from a lush wet jungle straight into a barren desert with cracks in the soil.

Eventually, she reached out and left me a long message on my voicemail. She simply said, "Hi dear, I'm sorry I haven't been in touch. I admit I was mad at you for not returning my messages, but then I put myself in your shoes and felt the overwhelm you must be feeling. And I thought – well, Beth doesn't have time or energy to call me back, I'll simply keep leaving her loving messages to let her know I'm here. So, I'm still here and love you very much, and can't imagine all you're going through. There's no need to call me back unless you can and want to."

Her words felt like fat drops of rain on parched soil. I started to cry and was relieved to know she was back in my inner circle of support. The world made sense for a short moment. This was another example of how cruel grief is by giving you more loss affected by the original loss. Keep showing up for your friends in crisis and know that right now the scales aren't balanced, but someday the scales may tip, and you will be the one in the crisis because we all end up in the grief club eventually. Actually, throw out the idea of balanced relationships. We simply need to help each other and forget about keeping score. Some people need more help than others. Fuck the idea of equal reciprocity and simply give when it's needed.

One day a friend texted this to me, "Hi Beth, thinking of you... What is Forrest Gump's password?"

I replied, "Hi, I have no idea what you're talking about, but it's nice to hear from you."

She quickly responded, "1forrest1."

I was surprised to hear from her because we weren't close at all, but many people were texting me at this time. Her text made me laugh and I enjoyed a moment of reprieve. She asked if it was okay to randomly send jokes to me a few times per week and I texted her back immediately and exclaimed, "Yes, keep 'em coming!"

Laughter and dark humor were super helpful even though there was nothing about our life to laugh about. Yet this was why laughter became one of my coping tools because when your life is shit, sometimes there's nothing else to do but laugh about it. My sense of humor became a superhero coping skill.

Other coping skills were simply nonexistent. It was just like my community—some familiar ones left, while others came closer. It was a confusing time, and I had to strive to find ways to keep going even when what helped me in the past no longer worked. And in the process, I was discovering a newfound inner strength from deep in my bones I didn't even know existed.

Somehow, I was able to rally to show up for Michael. My life's purpose became laser-focused on being strong to get through this. It showed up when I had no appetite but knew my body needed sustenance to keep going. I made myself eat the roasted chicken even though I didn't want to. I looked at my plate of food and said to myself, "That, (the food), must go in here (my mouth)."

It was as if all my Germans from Russia[4] ancestors were gathered around me saying, *du mus essen*. You must eat.

I started writing so as not to forget all the details and it led me to becoming the writer I am today. Writing was a creative outlet I needed to express myself in words. And I realized I was pretty good at it.

I started asking for help which provides others the opportunity to give. Eventually, I learned my burden was a gift, an invitation for others to show up. This is what true community is and we need to get back to this concept. Many people don't ask for help because they think they will be a burden on others. Before the accident, I took pride in doing everything on my own, but now I was learning about the beautiful interdependence of our existence.

I needed out-of-the-box ways to deal with my grief. What used to work with me no longer did. My usual ways of processing were journaling and drawing, after all, I was an art therapist. And art wasn't working for me. I felt stuck with it, and it also gave me more grief. I missed joy. I started following where I felt pulled to things that gave me more life and energy…and one of those things was shamanic journeying.

I attended a shamanic journey group event led by a shamanic practitioner in my local area. I arrived with my water bottle, a pillow and a blanket, my journal, an open heart, and lots of curiosity. After a brief explanation, we went into a shamanic journey practice. This kind of practice uses your imagination as you're invited to dive into a different world to receive visions and insights. It's done to a rapid rhythm of a drum beat to help you focus and guide you deeper. I had done this a few times pre-accident and would have a hard time dropping in. This time

---

[4] Germans from Russia – back in the 1760's Germans were invited to emigrate to Russia by the government of Catherine the Great. They lived there for two hundred years. They fled Germany in search of a life without poverty and famine. They went in search of a better life and were promised farmland. What they got was a harsh reality. They essentially went from one horrible situation to another. After learning about them, I have more awareness that my existence is an absolute miracle. Learn more about this at American Historical Society of Germans from Russia (https://ahsgr.org/)

I was there in an instant as if my soul was yearning for this experience. It's similar to dreaming and I was ready to travel to a different world, my healing world.

Here's what I wrote in my journal: *I dive down, safe place, into a pool, it turns to mud or shit? Falling into the underwater channels to a cenote and then I find myself in the salt flats or a desert. Then I meet them – the vulture and maggots. The vulture had one eye open, the other closed. They told me I'm still digesting this awful story of my life and I must trust it. I fly on them and then they eat me. I am shit out and then I fall. I am transmuted into white muck, like fresh bird shit. Now back on its wings, we fly. They show me their role is to eat death which is actually life. Are they now a dragon? Now I travel into the upper world where I meet the ENT trees from the Lord of the Rings movie. They offer their limbs like steps up to outer space. The dragon has a space suit and then turns into a spaceship. Then just me falling to gravity. The trees now hold a trampoline and I'm back up again until I'm weighted and swimming in outer space. The message: I'm my own alien; I'm an alien. And I must give hugs to each tree to say thank you.*

I love reading back on this journey. It reminded me to have patience and to trust the process Michael and I were going through. After Michael's accident, he seemed like an alien, and I felt like one too. The outer world felt odd – the sun rising the next day after the accident made no sense. I was angry at the sun and just wanted its intensity to stop. It would have felt totally normal if it had stayed dark for months. My world felt like I had been thrust into winter in the height of summer like I'd been catapulted to the other side of the planet. It was as if I was suddenly living in the middle of winter in the Northern Hemisphere, brought back to the land of my Scandinavian ancestors where they'd go for months without the sun. I held fast knowing my frozen life would begin to thaw at the first signs of spring. More importantly and unbeknownst to me I had signed up for a long deep apprenticeship with the dark.

Someone who had befriended the dark herself was my dear friend Raven. She came closer into my life. She was like the vulture who wasn't afraid of death and loss as she had been diving into her own death lodge experience at the time. Perhaps this was why she was able to support me easily and wasn't afraid of the shit I was covered with, just freshly out from the innards of the vulture.

Raven would break the rules on the dance floor of our ecstatic dance community where you weren't supposed to talk in the dance space. She would hold my shoulders and look me in the eyes and say, "You're in the depth of winter." And I would often collapse in a puddle of tears in her arms. She was a pillar of strength for me.

I kept dancing. I'd make myself go and was proud I did. I would go because Raven was there, and I'd seek her out on the dance floor. And then she would dance with me in whatever way I needed, which often didn't even look like dancing. Rather, it looked like she was casting out demons lodged in my lungs and deep in my bones. She would shake me, lay on top of me, vigorously massage all parts of me, make sounds into my heart and lungs or simply hold me while I cried or just sat there numb. My body craved these Raven grief healing sessions in the middle of the dance floor while everyone else was happily dancing and connecting with others. I felt out of place, yet I was exactly where I needed to be.

Dance! Dancing was a surprising coping tool that came closer in. And attending this dance weekly became part of my survival practice. The dance was part of a community in Denver called Rhythm Sanctuary which I'd been attending for many years before this. You were encouraged to communicate through your movement, body, voice, and throat. I became highly fluent in gibberish and the sounds of grief—I cried, wailed, keened, moaned, yelled, and screamed.

I would lay on the hardwood floor and shake, or I'd crawl under the large round tables which had been pushed aside at the Sons of Italy venue they would rent for this occasion. It was like going on a shamanic journey each time I stepped through the doorway, a portal to another world. It was a place where I could let my *Grief* do what she needed to do. She felt safe to come out in her black leather with her face covered in ash and be seen, heard, witnessed and held. She was touched, caressed, and danced. She was respected and allowed to be her full, raw, authentic self because you could do almost anything as long as you respected the space of others.

It's a Gabriel Roth *sweat your prayers* dance expression and my *Grief* and I loved it. Yet I also dreaded going. I'd make myself go. I'd drag myself to the dance and give myself permission to move my body the way it wanted. At times this meant I was a in heap of tears in the middle of the dance floor or under those tables. Attending the dance weekly became a priority, another lifeline or rather a grief line. Grief needs a through-line, just like birth does, except grief doesn't have an official midwife.

I was creating my own grief through-line; I became my own grief advocate. I found my friends who were able to come closer to me. Raven came in closer and became a grief midwife for me. Dancing was close, dancing was a midwife for me — making me move my body which helped me move my emotions which helped me move my grief. And this process was about birthing myself through the muck until I was able to rise up and out.

I kept searching for others who could help me and in July of 2014, I finally found a therapist. It was not easy to find her. It takes a lot to be a therapist's therapist. I had wanted to do a trauma protocol called "Eye Movement Desensitization and Reprocessing" (EMDR). I needed to process the vicarious trauma held in my body. Vicarious trauma, also known as secondary trauma, is when you take in the trauma of someone else. For me, this meant I kept seeing Michael's accident over and over, like a bad movie on repeat.

EMDR is a highly successful treatment for trauma and was first used on war veterans. The woman who created it, Dr. Francine Shapiro, found it after she went for a walk one day in San Francisco. She'd been processing something traumatic as she walked and when she returned, she noticed she felt much better. She began to question why – was it simply the act of walking or was it something else? As she was walking, she was thinking about her trauma and more importantly, her eyes were going from the left to the right while she was on the path. She did some research and discovered if you did bilateral eye movements while processing a trauma, eventually, the pain of the trauma would be desensitized.

My new therapist loved doing EMDR because it felt like doing a shamanic healing journey but instead of a drum it uses bilateral beats, taps, or buzzes. It made a lot of sense with my recent experience with my shamanic journey, and I was curious and eager to begin diving in. Yet I was also hesitant and scared to begin the process. There were times I was resistant and didn't want to dive into the trauma. She allowed me to go at my own pace, some days we didn't open up about the trauma and focused on other things I needed like talking about my sleep, self-care, and how my relationships were doing. There never was a time when I didn't have anything to talk about!

When looking for a therapist, I knew they needed to be well-versed in grief; they needed to have an awareness that it's not about getting closure or fixing it, or finding one's way back to normal. They also needed to have experience with the medical system and my therapist had been a chaplain at a hospital. Sitting in her office for the consultation, I remember seeing a small framed black chalkboard on a tiny easel, and on it were the words scrawled in white chalk: Love What Is. Before we had our conversation to see if we were a fit, I knew she was my therapist from just seeing those three words. Those three words had already been my mantra even way before this situation. Those words helped me after a shocking breakup with a man I thought I was going to be with for the rest of my life. That breakup put me in the pit of despair and depression, and I thought I'd hit rock bottom, until 2012, when a trap door opened and dropped me even deeper down. Love what is…three simple words, but those words can be the hardest concept to practice. I mean, how does one love losing their partner to quadriplegia?

CHAPTER 8

HOW TO LOVE QUADRIPLEGIA & SURGERY NUMBER TWO

"The human capacity for burden is like bamboo-
far more flexible than you'd ever believe at first glance."

—Jodi Picoult

To begin the daunting process of loving quadriplegia I had to learn more about it from the experts at Craig Hospital. Craig Hospital focuses on only two things – spinal cord injury and traumatic brain injury (SCI & TBI). We were especially grateful he only had one after meeting a patient in the elevator who had both.

Because Craig Hospital only focused on these two injuries, they were ranked as one of the best hospitals for these in the nation. And we were lucky enough to live just 39 miles away from it as it was located in Denver. He stayed at Craig Hospital for a bit over three months, ninety-five days or 136,800 minutes.

Michael had been in Longmont Hospital's ICU for 45 days and during this time the nurses and the CNAs were tracking his blood pressure

79

issue and weaning him off one particular drip med which stabilized him. As soon as he was no longer dependent on this, we could move from the ICU bed to the rehab bed at Craig Hospital. This weaning-off process is why it took us so long to go from one hospital bed to another.

Arriving at Craig Hospital for us was like thinking we'd arrived at our destination after a grueling hike and as we crested the hill, we discovered we had an entirely new mountain to climb. As we excitedly and apprehensively settled into our next home away from home, they ran a few tests to assess his physical situation, and we began to meet his new caregivers – doctors, nurses, CNAs, physical therapists, occupational therapists, and even a psychologist and a social worker. I was looking forward to us both finally getting some psychological and emotional support.

His new doctor, Dr. Xi (pronounced she, and he was a he and definitely not a she), came into the room to introduce himself, and then he delivered the worst news possible. In his impersonal and formal, straight-to-the-point, doctor speak he said, "I'm sorry Michael, there's a complication. C4 and C5 have not fused as they should've, and we'll need to do another surgery on your neck as soon as possible."

Fuck! What? We were simply shocked and beyond disappointed. Once again, I felt like I'd been punched in the gut. We were very excited to start this next chapter of rehab to learn how to live with this condition. But instead, we started with a sharp left turn as if we were on a road trip and had to navigate yet another detour.

The process got started immediately to check him into surgery at the adjoining facility called Swedish Hospital. I liked the name. It's where my ancestors come from. It had a cool gift shop where I bought my favorite mug which now holds my daily dose of coffee. The mug is decorated with simple Swedish folk art and the words, "*Var så god*," which literally means, 'Be so good,' 'You're welcome,' 'There you are,' and 'If it pleases you.' It pleased me because much of our life was the opposite of "*Var så god*."

I had to find things that brought me pure joy, and having a new mug with the language and art of my ancestors gave me a bit of this. I started becoming a joy detective; I made a daily practice to find the simplest joyful things, even if it was just for a moment.

We were devastated to hear he needed to undergo another full neck surgery. As if having the first one wasn't traumatic enough. The hardware inside his neck had fallen apart. Apparently, the first surgeon didn't use long enough screws. Remember my list from my orange notebook, the line that specifically said this: "Titanium screws and rods should last – won't get pulled out or torn because he won't be moving?"

Well, this was bullshit because those six screws did indeed move. And it made me wonder if this had happened when they transferred him from Longmont United to Craig Hospital. They transferred him by ambulance. He was strapped to a gurney. And I followed behind him in my little Rav 4 Toyota because otherwise I'd be stuck there without a car. I really wanted to be in the ambulance with him because I knew how hard this was on him.

Swedish Hospital was right next door to Craig Hospital and this was very intentional. In fact, you could get to it through what felt like a secret underground passageway in the very bottom of the basement – a wide yet low-ceilinged hallway connected the two hospitals. The ceiling was super low, even I could touch it – and I'm 5'2 ¾" tall!

Surgery number two was the next day, and it lasted the same amount of time as the first one – about eight hours. Dr. West, a spinal cord specialist who'd been in the field for more than ten years, worked on him. Our first surgeon had only been in her first year of actual practice. In hindsight, we should have had him transferred to Swedish Hospital for the first surgery and better care. But the very first day was intense. I simply rolled with the punches. We could have sued the first doctor but decided we were dealing with enough already – we didn't want to also engage in a legal battle. But sometimes I wonder if we should have as I could have directed all my rage into that.

While Michael was being prepped for his second surgery, I was entering one of Boulder's outdoor pools. A dear friend had signed me up as her unofficial nanny so I could receive the benefits of this pricey fitness club. I was grateful because their pool was filled with saline instead of chlorine. While Michael was going under anesthesia, I too was going under – under the water. I swam laps slowly while he was getting another set of neck hardware. I was doing self-care, while I let others be there for Michael. I imagined swimming in tears – mine and the ones from our community who had been greatly affected by his accident.

I'm a horrible swimmer, and I did laps next to the obsessed athletes Boulder is known for. I wasn't much of an athlete, and I wasn't much of a mountain biker either. I never really liked it. I owned a Schwinn mountain bike I bought back in 1996. I hardly ever used it on mountain trails. I used it to bike to work when I lived in Colorado Springs. I biked from Manitou Springs to north Colorado Springs, which was a hefty uphill commute. I feel proud about it now.

When I moved to Boulder in 1997 to study at Naropa University, I was invited to join one of my friend's boyfriends and a few of his buddies on a mountain bike ride. I said yes hesitantly. That morning I woke up with my period in full flow mode, but I went anyway. My body felt miserable, achy, and tired, but I wanted to prove I could do this. And I yearned for hanging out with the boys. It felt all too familiar growing up as the tomboy middle child between two brothers.

While going up the trail and over and through the rocks, like the rock that made my partner go up and over fifteen years later, my inner voice hollered to me, "What the hell are you doing and what are you trying to prove here? You can't even enjoy the scenery. You're not at this level of biking!"

I listened, got off my bike, and walked up and down the harder parts, which happened to be most of the parts. I knew then I wasn't a mountain biker and never would be. From then on, I only used my mountain bike to commute around the streets of Boulder. And to this day, this bike hangs in my garage collecting dust as I haven't ridden any kind of bike since the accident.

A few months before the accident I attempted to mountain bike with Michael because he loved it so much. He took me on a few easy rides near Boulder and taught me a few basic mountain biking skills. I was apprehensive yet willing to learn. And there were a few moments of pure joy when the riding was actually easy. I do remember seeing him lose his balance as he was trying to go up and over large rocks and he almost fell over backward. It gave me quite a scare!

A few months later in June of 2012, we took a trip to Moab to be with my parents and both of my brothers, their wives, and my six nephews. Michael, my sister-in-law Michelle, two of my nephews and I went on a beginner trail. I felt excited, proud, and nervous to be getting on my mountain bike again as it'd been about 15 years since I last rode it for its original purpose. After all, they call it a "mountain bike." As I was rounding a sharp corner I fell and scraped my elbow badly. Michael was ahead of me and was poised on a rock to take my photo so he didn't see me fall. Instead, he saw me slowly biking towards him with a shocked expression on my face and refrained from taking my photo and tended to me instead. Afterward, while he was driving us back to our Airbnb, he made me laugh to diffuse the trauma in my body. Looking back, it's eerily ironic, because two months later we'd switch positions and I'd be the one helping him laugh off his trauma.[5]

Back in the pool on the day of his second surgery, there was a very pregnant woman swimming, and I was even slower than her. I didn't care. The accident rid me of my judgmental self – I didn't care what I looked like or how I was swimming. I simply swam as a prayer, and I didn't care about my form or if I was getting my heart rate up. I just needed to be in the water to keep my body moving which helped me keep my internal process moving too. My emotions flowed with each puny stroke I made while I added a few more tears to the saline pool.

---

[5] Michael had studied with Annette Goodheart, Ph. D. She developed Laughter Therapy and wrote a book entitled, *Laughter Therapy: How to Laugh About Everything in Your Life That Isn't Really Funny.*

Having the ability to attend this club was such a gift to me, yet it was also bizarre. At first, I thought no one knew me, but I soon realized a lot of my friends could afford this club. I would occasionally run into them there and have awkward conversations while naked and getting dressed. It's a great metaphor for grief– being naked and getting dressed around acquaintances – vulnerability and rawness out for everyone to see.

I sought privacy in the fancy shower stalls, the ones with the rain shower heads which make it feel as if you're in the middle of a monsoon. It often felt like I had my personal dark rain cloud hovering above me everywhere I went. I knew it was there, but others didn't. I cried often in the shower stall. As the water lingered down my body like tiny rivers, I could only dwell on Michael and all we had lost. Life was just strange – it was hard to listen to other women in the locker room complain about First World problems and/or normal life challenges. Many people don't realize how good they have it until it's gone. Like me, I took sex for granted, holding hands, cuddling, dancing, hiking, driving, going on road trips, and even arguing. All those normal able-body activities you do together as a couple.

While I was in the pool attempting to swim laps, others were supporting Michael. His buddy Joel came to visit. They'd met 20+ years ago when Michael was working as an engineer at Kodak. They had this thing about calling each other Dude and would send each other cards with 'dude' in the message. When they called each other, they'd start the call with a big, long, "Duuuuude!"

Michael's oldest sister Julie was there too. At the time, she had been living in Saudi Arabia where her husband was working. She flew all the way to be here to support her brother. Julie was a fierce mama bear and took her advocacy work seriously when it came to Michael's health. While this was appreciated and needed, she was at the same time very challenging to be around for me.

Since the J team, Joel and Julie, were there to help, I decided to let others hold him close while I held my self-care closer. I felt immense guilt at the time for doing this, but I was also coming to realize my life was now a marathon and I needed others to run it for me. Or rather, my life was more like a relay race, and I needed to hand off the caregiving baton in order to care for myself. Eventually, this would be something I would have to lean into and learn much more about to be able to care for him and myself for the long haul.

The surgery, although long, went smoothly. Seeing him post-surgery number two was extremely difficult. The lighting in his room was dim like you were fireside in a cave, which was nice, but otherwise, it was hard to see him again in a large amount of pain. He was in much more pain than the first surgery which had only been 51 days prior. He didn't have Michael Jackson's white lightning and the nurses weren't as sweet; I missed Rhonda, the mama bear nurse. Maybe it was harder this time because it was his second neck surgery, and his body hadn't even healed properly from the first one. Or maybe I was learning there was nothing I could do to relieve his pain. There's nothing worse than seeing your loved one in physical pain knowing there's nothing you can do to change it.

Michael stayed at Swedish for a few days to recover and then they brought him back to Craig Hospital through the secret underground passageway. He started his rehab process recovering from surgery, which wasn't the plan. Honestly, none of this was part of the plan. And did we even have a plan at this point other than just get through each moment, each day and keep going? Another mantra that held me steady was "Keep calm, carry on." This phrase comes from England during WWII to increase morale during wartime. It made sense because I did feel as if my nervous system was under attack. I wouldn't use that phrase to bypass whatever was happening, I used it to remind myself to try to keep going forward calmly.

Back at Craig...Dr. Xi wasn't the most pleasant man to deal with, but he was an excellent physician. When I think back about him, I see one painful and weird memory. I was about to go into the room to see Michael, and at this point, Michael had C-diff, a very contagious bacterial infection and you had to wear disposable yellow robes and gloves to even enter the room and when you left the room you had to take them off immediately. I was dressed for the part and about to enter when one of his nurses asked me to come and see something on the computer screen in the nurses' station. I followed her in my yellow robe. And little did I know I was doing two things very wrong.

When Dr. Xi saw me, all dressed in yellow, he came at me like a madman, grabbed my robe, ripped it off of me, and proceeded to yell at me in his gruff and angry monotone voice, "You're not supposed to be in here and you shouldn't be wearing this. Take it off and get out!"

I wished he could have simply ripped out and taken off this entire experience. But that wasn't possible. Instead, I stood there flabbergasted, I felt slightly naked, even though I had clothes on under the yellow robe. I felt blasted and violated and it felt as if I was suddenly wearing a puke green color robe of shame instead. Yet, I didn't know the rules.

I steered way clear of Dr. Xi after this, and I was careful the next time I was allowed into the nurses' station. Being allowed into command central fed the adolescent part of me who just wanted to rebel and do things wrong on purpose. I took photos of Michael's X-rays from the nurses' computer screen with my phone. I did it once and was told I couldn't so then I did it a few other times.

Being in such grief and trauma gave me this weird sense of entitlement. I ran through red lights late at night a few times and did the slight tap on the pedal at stop signs, thinking the usual societal rules no longer applied to me. It was as if this situation gave me the go-free pass. This didn't last long as the more logical part of me took over and reminded me we didn't need to deal with another kind of accident or tragedy. And the therapist part of me was relieved when I changed my unhealthy behavior.

There were a few things I did love about Craig Hospital. They treated you like family, usually. Instead of stiff white nurses and doctor's coats, the staff wore casual clothes to make you feel like you were at home unless you have C-diff. Although I seem to remember Dr. Xi being slightly stiff and very impersonal no matter what kind of clothes he wore.

When Michael was at Longmont United Hospital at the beginning, life was easier. There was ease in my body knowing he was mostly well taken care of by the nurses and staff. Then when he moved to Craig Hospital I had even more ease in my body knowing he was super supported by doctors, nurses, PTs and OTs, and everyone else with trained expertise in all things related to quadriplegia. I no longer had to doubt their knowledge.

Time at Craig Hospital was hard though. Even though the staff was better equipped to handle SCI, there were many things I hated about it. It was like my life—many things were sweet and many things were just fucking bitter.

I remember driving up to see Michael after I had spent time with my parents in Colorado Springs. I drove under the sky bridge which was partly made of glass for the patients at Craig Hospital to view the outside world. From my car, I could see him on the sky bridge and was excited to see him up and out of his room. I yelled up to him even though I knew he couldn't hear me. I drove closer and saw his gaze. I was trying to reach him as we could often sense the other's presence, or we'd say the same thing at the exact same time. I thought I could reach him, but he was far away – he was sullen, frozen and in the deepest depressive state I'd ever seen. He shared later that he was looking at people walking easily on the sidewalk – going up the curbs and getting into their cars. He saw the ones with paraplegia, who are paralyzed from the waist down and have use of their upper bodies. He said, "I never imagined I'd be jealous of paraplegics, oh how I wish I had the use of my arms and torso like they do."

We were both very depressed. Michael was learning and adjusting to being in his new body. And I was adjusting as well. Yet I didn't let others see my depressed state and especially Michael, I tried to stay positive for him yet stay in touch with my emotions. Our time at Craig Hospital helped us with the transition physically and mentally. And they attempted to help us emotionally but failed in my opinion. If I were to give them a grade, I would give them D+.

Craig Hospital was one of the top hospitals in the nation for traumatic brain and spinal cord injuries and they far exceeded what we needed medically and physically. However, the social-emotional support we got was pathetic. I attended the psycho-educational support group when my busy schedule allowed me to be there, which wasn't that often. They would often show videos and the first one we saw together talked about the perks of having a spinal cord injury. Right?! Perks. And you know what they described first? Close-up parking to all the venues because of disability. (And actually, this is not true as we often go somewhere and all the accessible parking is taken. There are more people with disabilities than the ADA parking requirements require.)

Because I was trained as a therapist, I expected this to be a group with emotional support and grief work about how to deal with this intense transition from being an able-bodied person to one who's disabled. This was not the case. Instead, they covered topics like how to deal with his pee bag, nutrition, and a bit about changes in your sexual life. All important info, but I needed emotional support and I thought they were going to cover this in the group.

The best emotional support I got was when I was introduced to a woman whose husband had also been at Craig Hospital. She was a friend of my parents' friends. Her husband had been hit by a garbage truck one morning on his bike commute to work. We shared a similar experience – of not having our emotional needs met there. From her, I learned 75% of marriages split after a spinal cord injury. This is a very high number. Our first meeting was a very long lunch because we couldn't stop sharing our stories. It was really helpful to find someone in similar shoes. We only met twice but I found it meant the world to me to be speaking my two new languages – grief AND quadriplegia: a different kind of bilingual-ness.

When you suddenly find yourself in the world of SCI a lot of support is needed. I wonder how the support group is doing now. I no longer need this, but I really could have used it then. In fact, what I really needed was a grief support group run by someone, not at the beginning of their journey with it. And I wanted to scream back then...*can we name the fucking elephant in the room please – Grief and Trauma?* They were there like characters following us around everywhere, like *Shock* who was sucking on those chicken bones on that fateful first night.

Now they were like unseen ghosts in the hallways, in patients' rooms, and even in the closets. The coziest closet at Craig Hospital was the one specifically for keeping blankets warm. Michael could ask for a warm blanket any time. He couldn't regulate his temperature[6], this was one of the things he had to adjust to—being cold most of the time. Those warm blankets felt like a blanket taken out of the dryer. Reminds me of my childhood, my mom used to throw the clothes on us straight out of the dryer and demand we fold them. I'd be watching cartoons and she'd dump the basket of clothes on top of me. I would enjoy the warm sensation for a moment and then we'd get to work, me and my brothers, folding our family's array of underwear and jock straps. (I grew up with two brothers who were both athletes. I was the middle artsy child).

Another thing Craig didn't do well was work with local families and partners. Since Craig is known nationwide, most of its patients were flown in from out of state to be there. We lived less than an hour away depending on traffic. This meant I was also attempting to keep my private practice up and running. At times, I felt like Superwoman. I would often get annoyed though because they'd schedule meetings with doctors or support staff without checking in with me. I spoke up one day and asked them to consult with me first to set up meetings so I could be there. I gave them suggestions of better times for me. But this was a pipe dream...especially when it came to the medical meetings. I had to rearrange my schedule often. I got angry each time. And it made me feel as if I didn't matter and the medical doctors were the ones leading the

---

[6] A person with paralysis, quadriplegia, paraplegia, cannot sweat below their level of injury, thus their body cannot regulate their temperature through sweating.

show. They had a lot of power over us. It wasn't inclusive treatment, at least not to me.

The D+ support group went on a few outings. One day they did a huge one — they took the bus to see a movie and go out to dinner afterward. I was bummed I couldn't rearrange my schedule, so Michael's sister Linda went with him. She said it was fun to go out with Michael as it was the first time he'd been out since the accident. She enjoyed being with him outside of the confines of the hospital, but Michael had a hard time with it. And I did too even though I wasn't there. It was his first time being out in the world as an obviously disabled person. It was where people saw the wheelchair first and him as a person second.

To me, this outing was epic for this reason, and I thought we'd discuss it from the emotional perspective in the next support group. We did not. And I was stunned, shocked really. There was no emotional support for the grief and loss of suddenly becoming quadriplegic. I couldn't believe it and I started rewriting the social-emotional program for Craig Hospital in my head.

There were a lot of firsts post-accident. The first time he was able to sit upright in a chair, the first time he went outside (sometime in September), he was able to feel the sun on his face and feel the fresh air on his body where he could feel it, which was any area above the nipples. Other firsts were the first time he had shit running down his legs, the first time he called me on the phone, and the first time I heard his voice after having a tube down his throat. The first time he ate real food…which brought us to another medical crisis…the tracheostomy. Remember that one?

One month into our three-month stay at Craig, I had a one-on-one appointment with the woman who led the psycho-social groups, and I asked if there was a caregiver support group. She replied without hesitation perhaps because she knew I was a therapist, "No, how about starting one?"

I must have had a deer-in-the-headlights look because her words punctured me as if she'd slapped me in the face. Her response was far from helpful. I was immediately angry, and my inner voice screamed,

"Are you fucking kidding me? You want me to start a support group when I'm in the middle of needing it myself?"

I left feeling angry, very sad, and utterly disappointed, knowing the person who was trained to help us deal with these social/emotional challenges, did not fully understand my needs. This department was lacking big time.

Around this time, I started tuning into something larger than myself. I was walking down the wider-than-usual hallway, wider to accommodate the chunky power wheelchairs and smaller manual ones. And I heard a voice in my head say to me, "Beth, pay attention to all this…it's going to come in handy someday."

I heard this thought and tucked it away because I needed to pay attention to everything going on – the inner and outer workings which were working on all of us. This voice is now known as my *Entrepreneur-Healer-Higher-Self*, the one who takes charge and is always thinking about how to use experiences to help others with grief. I love this part of me— she was smart as a whip and her suggestion was great. She was sophisticated and wore a white linen tunic, black pants with a dark red leather jacket. She looked great next to *Shock* in her black leather pants. They walked side by side now. I agreed it would come in handy as I imagined I might be helping others navigate medical situations or vicarious trauma like this someday.

CHAPTER 9

MEET MY ANGER, MY INNER DRAGON

"Rage became a layer of my skin."

—Soraya Chemaly

However, I was in no way able to help others or lead a support group as I was still in the acuteness of the tragedy and dealing with too much; I was still wrestling with quadriplegia. Not with Michael, but with the idea itself. Instead of fighting it, I was struggling with loving it and grappling with how to accept our new reality.

One thing which was wrestling with me was how inaccessible our home was at the time of the accident. We had been living in a three-story townhome, it had more height than width – it went up alongside the ponderosa pine tree and created shade for the dilapidated and abandoned hammock which was a home for the squirrels. And on the fateful accident day, Michael's family booked their flights as soon as they knew he was injured. They didn't even ask to stay with me in our home, it was simply assumed. And I realized why we lived there after the accident happened—we had more than enough space to accommodate everyone comfortably.

I suddenly became housemates with my in-laws – his parents Armand and Bonnie stayed for a few weeks and his sister, Linda, and her husband Greg were able to stay about six months. Greg was working remotely, and Linda wasn't working so she was able to devote her time to helping us navigate this new life. I was grateful for their help as there was no way I could have done this alone. Suddenly we became a family, and I wasn't bothered at all by this, I needed the help and was happy to share our three-story home.

Eventually, Linda and Greg brought their cat, Willow, to live with us. I was hesitant about this at first, having to deal with a pet deposit and coming to grips with the idea I had never lived with a cat. In the end, I was so happy about this as I fell in love with their kitty. We became instant playmates; she helped me laugh and be fully present in the moment. She helped me love stairs again. I hated them because Michael would never walk up or down them ever again. But with Willow, I loved those stairs and how we got lost in time playing together. It became our nightly ritual I looked forward to.

It was these stairs which became an issue with the worst-ever rental company in my opinion. Ironically, their name is associated with sunshine. They were far from sunny and they should be called Slumlord or Asshole Management Company. Actually, I take that back, my asshole does a duty I used to take for granted and it's now a part of my body I highly appreciate. I'll explain more about my asshole in a bit…

The "sunny" company decided to charge us a fee to get out of the lease early. This meant we wouldn't get our deposit back. The fee and our deposit equaled the amount equivalent to double the rent. And we had no choice but to break the lease – Michael couldn't live there! This mushroomed into an unwanted conflict. It was December of 2012, while Michael was still in rehab at Craig Hospital.

A friend suggested I hire a lawyer. As if my life wasn't complicated enough already, now I had to deal with legal issues. I found an organization in Denver that provides pro bono legal assistance for people with disabilities. Turns out the rental company was legally obligated to make accommodations so Michael could live there. The lawyers wrote a simple letter saying—you either have to make the unit accessible for Michael (build many ramps & install elevators) or allow them to break the lease early without a fine.

I arranged a meeting to discuss this with someone at the rental company. I showed up with the letter to back me up. I was really nervous about my appointment. I did a pep talk with myself in my car and took a few deep breaths. Then I walked in and started explaining the situation to the person assigned to help me. The owner overheard our conversation. He was very tall and had thick black hair. He was suddenly towering over us. Looking down at me, he rudely said in a staccato angry tone, "Why didn't you call me? You didn't have to bring the law into this!"

I wanted to jump on him like Golum or another evil angry creature and scream this into his ear, "You fucking asshole! How dare you charge us another month's rent because my partner is suddenly a quadriplegic and can no longer live there and walk up and down all those fucking stairs! You're a scum landlord and I'll tell everybody I know never to rent from you!"

But I didn't. I simply tightened my lips and braced my body to speak my truth. And without hesitation, I stood up and looked him straight in the eyes and simply said, "I did call you, in fact, I called you a few times and left you messages. You never replied which is why I brought legal action into this."

Once again fierce honesty was fueling me forward. I don't have room for bullshit anymore and can see through it like I'd acquired superpowers. I was no longer afraid to speak my truth. It was both beautiful and ugly at the same time.

After my strong and clear statement, we were able to discuss our situation, and I was finally heard. The letter from the lawyer did indeed help resolve it and we were able to get out of the lease and not be charged double rent. Part of me just wanted some compassion from them and from other strangers I encountered. Why is it hard to say, "I'm so sorry you're in this predicament." Followed by, "Let's figure out something which works for all of us?" In the end, it's about business and making money, not human connection and compassion. And this made me sad.

After the meeting, I got in my car, my tiny dark green home on wheels; that had held me through many a breakdown and many a grief burst. I took a moment to sit there – to cry and scream even though the outcome of the meeting was good. I screamed very loud. I even frightened myself because I'd never screamed like this before. I had an enormous amount of fucking rage at the rental property manager, at our situation, at the accident, having to move, having to find an accessible home, and having to deal with everything regarding Michael suddenly becoming a quadriplegic. I was forced to learn how to take care of a grown man as if he were an infant. I was full of bitter jealousy at my two girlfriends who had just had babies and were now enjoying mothering them. It felt utterly cruel; it was too much, and I was cracking open.

Yes, there definitely was a crack, growing like a chasm, my emotions unearthed and bubbling to the surface. It seemed they were arriving all at once. You know all those "stages" of grief, right? They are most commonly known as denial, anger, bargaining, depression, and acceptance. Well, they're really intertwined together at times like one big, tangled knot. And there are many more emotions and they don't come all nicely packaged in stages. Stages imply a chronological order and then you'll eventually be done and move on. Wouldn't that be nice? Well, grief isn't linear, according to Francis Weller, it's feral. And it comes and goes as it pleases in any form it wants.

Those stages of grief come from Dr. Elizabeth Kubler-Ross who was a pioneer in the world of palliative care. She fought to go to medical school when women weren't allowed to and started practicing medicine in the 1950s and 60s. Her practice led her to work with the dying and eventually, she helped start the hospice movement in the United States.

The stages of grief were from her research she did with people who were dying, not the ones left behind who were grieving. Somehow these stages became about the grief process. Later I learned from my grief mentor, Alan Wolfelt, she regretted using the word "stages" to describe the dying process. Interestingly, she died on the anniversary of my birthdate on August 24th, 2004. Her biography was one of the many books I read about grief at the beginning of all this and I came away with more appreciation for her pioneering personality and groundbreaking work in the hospice movement.

I was in the process of getting to know all my emotions and befriending them and ultimately inviting them into my sense of home. The one 'stage' I connected to the most was anger. It moved in without asking, it just plowed through my door and showed up often followed by rage.

Many people don't know how to handle anger – their own or the expression of it in others. Anger is a great teacher – it shows up when our boundaries have been violated. Rage is worse in my opinion, and according to Francis Weller, rage is a wounded reactivity to injury or insult. Rage to me feels off the rails, whereas anger feels like it stays within the guardrails. I was in the process of going on and off the road, a different kind of road rage.

I would express my anger and rage appropriately and other times not. I had to learn how to express myself better when it showed up. Eventually, I learned to recognize when I was getting upset and would take care of it by moving the five end points of my body – my arms, legs, and my throat. I learned this from Annie Brook. And moving the five-end points makes sense, right? I mean what do you want to do when you're really angry? I want to hit, kick and scream. I started imagining my anger was like a dragon who lived inside my belly and when I started to feel her waking up, I'd take her for quick walks when she needed to spit fire at the world.

I often wanted to spit fire at just about anyone and anything. I did this with strangers, friends, and family. I'd even get angry at curbs and stairs and anything inaccessible – even innocent rocks on the trail, especially the one that caused the accident. Most of the world isn't accessible and until you're either dealing with a disability like this or know someone who does, you won't really have this awareness.

My anger and rage were rooted in my loss of control in my life and losing too much in a short amount of time. I was angry often and it seemed there was more and more piling on to what I was already dealing with. I would also come to learn that it was easier for me to be mad than sad; sadness showed my vulnerability.

The first time I met my anger and rage was when I saw Michael's bike after the accident. My dad and good friend Marty, my friend Linda's former partner, and father to Hannah, my goddaughter, and the most reliable and loyal person I know went to retrieve Michael's car and bike where it was left behind at the trailhead parking lot. They were bringing it up those fucking stairs from the parking lot. Yes, there were even stairs from the parking lot, followed by stairs up to our porch, then inside the front door, there were stairs going up and stairs to go down two levels. We had an abundance of stairs, and I had an abundance of anger that I couldn't contain.

When I saw his bike, I felt as if I'd been suddenly knocked over, and without hesitation, I let out strange sounds which were part screams and part sobs as I yelled, "I don't want to see that fucking bike!"

Both Marty and my dad looked at me with compassion, concern, and their own grief and shock. Then Marty asked me calmly, "What should we do with it?"

The dragon within awakened instantly and my words came out like fire, "Put it in the fucking garage, I don't wanna see it ever again!"

And I didn't, we sold it a few months later for a fair price. After all, it was a really nice low-weight high-end mountain bike. Michael didn't hold back with his budget on things he loved and valued like biking, traveling, and training to be a better practitioner. Michael spent money easily in this way, compared to me and my miserly ways; he spent, I saved. We differed in how we used money.

I got to know my dragon within really well. I began to see a pattern – it would start with irritation and frustration and then it would build until she breathed out fire at anyone or anything in her path.

I got annoyed at something small once and I turned to my parents who were there helping me at the time. I placed my pointer finger across my lips and said, "Shush, don't wake the dragon, she's waking up, don't take anything I say or do personally in the next thirty minutes. I'm going for a walk to see if I can put her back to sleep."

They looked at me slightly bewildered yet understood I needed to go take care of myself. I learned to walk and move when I started to feel frustrated so the tiny spark of irritation wouldn't become a raging out-of-control fire.

My emotional process wasn't graceful, especially in the beginning. I would explode on strangers, or the apartment complex management, or the Verizon Wireless person who insisted they had to talk to Michael directly to change something on our account. I freaked out and explained he was unable to talk because he was attached to medical devices keeping him alive in the ICU.

At one point during the first few months, a friend of mine was scared by my anger as I later learned she and another good friend were talking about me. She said to the other, "Beth is so angry lately, it's hard to be around her."

And my friend Merryl, who is also a Grief Warrior herself, defended me and said, "She has every right to be angry – she just lost her life partner to quadriplegia and they're now suddenly thrust into a life with a disability. Of course, she's angry!"

She shared this with me later, and I appreciated her sticking up for me. And when I learned my other friend couldn't handle my anger, of course, it made me angry.

One of the things which was hard was I felt like I had no place for the anger and rage to go. I was angry at Michael only for a moment... because how could I be mad at him for doing what he loved to do? He loved mountain biking and when he crashed, he was just doing what he loved. Then I was mad at his fancy bike. Then I was mad at the rock he hit and the trail he was on. I was even mad at Earth for the phenomena of gravity which pulled him down.

I was also mad at myself for not telling him to come home for dinner. I should have asked him to ride his bike on another night. Monday nights were our time to be together before he went off to Fort Collins for a few days. Shoulda, coulda, woulda —they always seemed to be followed by immense guilt. My anger suddenly switched to guilt for not asking him to stay home. I was all over the place with my emotions. And I would loop in my thoughts — could I have saved him from this if I had demanded he come home for dinner?

I was also angry at God or whatever higher power existed for letting this happen, which didn't feel right either. Instead of directing my rage at them, I raged at every little thing that went wrong, which happened often.

By now I said fuck many times a day and I didn't even care who heard me either. It's the language anger and rage speak, and apparently, I was becoming pretty fluent. I later learned having a potty mouth can actually help relieve stress. If you're upset, angry, or stressed, let it fucking rip!

I cussed often about how I had to find us an accessible home; I was often in denial about this. It was a daunting task to find an appropriate home. It was no easy feat because Michael no longer had the use of his feet. And I just wanted to rewind and go back to when our life was normal and easy. I would pray for ease; I'd yell at God or the universe to just give me a fucking break. Yes, I'd swear at God. I guess I was directing some of my anger at them. At this point, everything felt like an uphill battle, and I was getting really tired.

Everything seemed to be hitting me all at once. I was dealing with Michael in two hospital stays — first at Longmont United then at Craig Hospital. During our stay at Craig, I was juggling all this: working and seeing the minimum of clients to keep my private practice going, learning all I could about living with quadriplegia – both mentally and emotionally. I was showing up for Michael at the hospital, navigating living with his family, trying to get adequate sleep and rest, and taking care of myself. I was also dealing with changes in my other relationships, and so many other secondary losses. And then, on top of it all, I was just trying to tend to normal life things like paying bills, feeding myself, doing laundry, and on and on.

I couldn't get a break. And I continued to yell at God and the Universe to just give me a fucking break and send some ease my way. I yelled in the car, no surprise there, and I even hit the passenger seat while driving. After this, I would pull over to scream, wail, and sob. I had to learn to tame this dragon!

There were times I missed my old and uneventful pre-accident life. And now when I feel bored, I say a prayer of gratitude. As my friend Lisa Hunter's song called "Nuthin" says, "I would rather have nothing than a little bit of something wrong."

Too much of my life was just utterly wrong.

I was beyond stressed, and I wanted this marathon to end or at least slow down. I fantasized often about putting the world on pause just to catch up. I had too much to deal with, too much grief to process, I felt as if I was running behind everyone else's more normal lives.

But I had to keep going. And part of the never-ending marathon was looking for a home while Michael was still in rehab at Craig Hospital. Michael couldn't come home until we found an accessible one. He never returned to the townhouse where we had only lived together for about nine months. The hospitals had become our home. It felt oddly official when I put LUH as a contact in my phone, (LUH=Longmont United Hospital), and then later I added Craig Hospital. And I want to remind you we stayed in the first hospital for forty-five days and then we were at Craig for ninety-six days. It did feel like our home – it became our central hub where we spent most of our time. But we knew we couldn't stay there forever, nor would we want to. I only wanted to because everything was much easier when I had a team of people well-versed in the ways of SCI always around to help Michael with his many needs.

In some ways, the beginning was much easier on me even though Michael was suffering more. My nervous system could relax slightly because I knew he had a team of nurses, CNAs, and doctors always available to him. I felt guilty for feeling this. It was easier too because it meant the place I lived was not inundated with caregivers and medical staff; it was still my home.

CHAPTER 10

FINDING HOME

*"I'd cut my soul into a million different pieces just to form a
constellation to light your way home. I'd write love poems to the parts of
yourself you can't stand. I'd stand in the shadows of your heart and tell
you I'm not afraid of your dark."*

—Andrea Gibson

Home. What does it mean really? And what does it mean to be at
"home" in your own body – your flesh, skin, and bones? I suppose
this entire story is about coming home or finding home as a couple again
with each other radically changed on many levels. Tragedy blew us both
wide open and then we sat and watched the pieces fall to the ground
around us. We were doing the daunting task of taking inventory of our
old life combined with these new parts. We had to ask what fit and what
didn't. Then we had to love what was and find some kind of semblance
of the chaos; the chaos which was part of this new life.

The end of our time at our home away from home, aka Craig
Hospital, was stressful. Before we were officially discharged, they moved
us to an independent apartment across the street, but still a part of Craig

Hospital, where we were required to do all of Michael's care without any of their assistance for two weeks. For us, this happened at one of the most challenging times of the year – the holidays and in the middle of winter. We would be moving from the hospital in mid-January.

Michael's sister Linda and I were undergoing the worst "hands-on" test ever. We had to do everything ourselves – get him out of bed and into his chair, do his stretching routine, feed him, give him his meds, brush his teeth, shower him, shave him, do his bowel program, change his catheter, and anything else he needed. Essentially, I had to learn skills taught in nursing school. I felt as if I was working on an unofficial nursing degree, and I even added this later to my curriculum vitae under the category of "other life experiences that matter."

Doing his bowel program for the first time on my own was etched into my brain. It was on New Year's Eve, 2012. We didn't celebrate unless you consider me putting my finger into his anus to do what they call "stimming" a celebration. (Well, it could be for some). Kneeling behind him facing the corner of the shower room, him in the commode chair strapped in case he had a spasm and fell out, I was doing what I'd been taught to do to remind his body it was time to defecate. I never thought I'd take pooping for granted nor did I think I'd come to appreciate assholes like I do now. I'm very aware of how amazing and convenient it is to be able to take a shit in a few minutes vs an hour or two depending on how his body responds and how much shit gets elsewhere. This is why I have a newfound appreciation of the asshole, and I think twice about calling someone that now.

That New Year's Eve is one I'll never forget. Sticking my finger up his asshole I thought to myself, well this isn't how I thought I'd be doing this. I'd imagined doing this for a different kind of reason, a sexual purpose to be utterly honest. It was a sad moment, with the saddest part being the fact Michael couldn't feel any of it, and instead of feeling the possibility of pleasure, he actually fell asleep.

Those two weeks doing all his care was hard but necessary. We had to do this so the Craig Hospital staff knew and more importantly, we knew we could do this on our own at home. Then we could be officially discharged and sent on our way to start the next "leg" of the journey. Where did that expression come from? The next leg of the journey was difficult. And I really missed Michael's able-bodied legs.

This was an unbearable time and thankfully Michael's sister, Linda, was there to help me carry this load of being his full-time caregiver. At the time she was in her early fifties. She's the middle child of three with Michael being the youngest. She and Michael have a close relationship, they talked often and supported each other. She is slender like Michael. They both had trouble putting on weight throughout their lives. They even look alike; it is obvious they are siblings.

Linda is an herbalist and can grow anything anywhere as all ten digits were green, not just her thumbs. She has an intensity about her at times which was challenging to be around for me. We clashed a few times while living together but for the most part, we became quite close through all this, and we learned how to repair when conflict arose.

I was grateful for her because she helped me yank my head out of the sand in which it was stuck. One of our biggest clashes was when she addressed my full-on denial about finding a place for us to live. I was rejecting the reality of looking for a new place to live which would meet Michael's needs. Again, it was like my mind was telling me if I didn't deal with it, it wasn't happening. Denial is just weird at times. But it's also beneficial as it can give you a much-needed break or distraction in order for you to catch up and handle your grief or just take a breather; it's a possible pause button. Yet it can be detrimental and cause more problems when you're not dealing with reality.

One day in the middle of December, I was enjoying the occasional mild weather days we are blessed with in Colorado where we can wear t-shirts instead of parkas. Linda called me on the phone while I was just sitting in my car with the window down, trying to have some private alone time away from the constant interruptions at Craig Hospital. Which brings up more grief – loss of any alone time with my partner. Hospital staff would walk into his room at any time. As a result, I was spending more and more time in my sweet car; it held me well and felt like a home on wheels.

Linda said excitedly, "Beth, we found a few accessible places and made appointments for you to see them."

I said nothing.

She said, "Beth? Are you there?"

"Yes, I'm here. Thanks, but I don't have time to do that," I said with a descending out breath.

She immediately replied in a slightly frustrated and staccato tone, "Beth, when are you going to do this? You only have a few weeks left until you need a place for you and Michael. It's not about doing this when you want to and is convenient for your schedule. You have to make time for this!"

I was annoyed and didn't want to be told what to do. I wanted to run away and put my head in the sand where it was comfortable. Or at least go put my feet in the sand and stay there awhile. I begrudgingly said, "Okay, I'll go see one place before I go to work today."

And it was very frustrating to go and see these supposed "accessible" units. Many places claimed they were accessible and ADA compliant, (ADA stands for Americans with Disabilities Act). We learned just because a place claims it's accessible doesn't mean it truly is. Disability falls on a spectrum with some needs accommodated easily and others not. Quadriplegia falls on the more challenging side of the spectrum and some aspects of a place to live just wouldn't be accessible for our unique needs.

For instance, the bathroom layouts were often just wrong. We'd miss the huge bathroom (10' x 10') at Craig Hospital where the entire floor and most of the walls were covered in tile. It makes it much easier to clean up shit that seems to get everywhere. I swear I think CNAs must take a course on how to manage shit and not get it all over everything. The art of poop cleanup is real, and it needs lots of practice.

The tile walls at Craig Hospital remind me of our travels in Europe. Michael and I once found this cute place on the coast of Portugal. We were there in June of 2010. It was our first trip abroad together of what we thought would be many. We had made a list of places we wanted to go: Argentina, Cuba, Italy, and Greece…

We were driving down a narrow dirt road in the late afternoon and saw two adorably cute older Portuguese women in the street. They both looked as if they enjoyed eating and were dressed in a mishmash of colors – skirts, aprons, and scarves on their heads like they were ready to get to work in their home or garden. We stopped to say hello and they asked us in broken English if we needed a place to stay. And we did. They had a place for us, and we were thrilled. They were getting ready to clean it and told us to return in two hours. It was quaint, yet open and modern and it had a view of the ocean but only if you stood on your tiptoes at the kitchen window, well, at least I had to stand on my tip toes to see it. The bathroom was tiled from floor to ceiling in beautiful dark brown sparkly tiles. We talked about wanting to do this in our bathroom in a house we'd call home someday.

I wish finding our new place had been as easy as finding the place in Portugal with two colorful older women pointing to it. It wasn't as delightful or easy. When I arrived to see the apartment Linda had arranged, I was dubious. She and Greg met me in the parking lot to view it with me. It was one of those fancy apartment complexes with all the amenities and a signature smell wafting out of these timed machines in the hallways. It had all the perks for able bodies – a pool, a workout space, co-working spaces, and a community room with specialty coffees and even a bar. It was definitely not us. But again, I had no choice, I had to find someplace for us to live.

A young woman with too much makeup on and smelling of strong perfume showed us the place. This is where my fierce honesty made another appearance. I was just tired of being shown "accessible" places only to learn they were far from it. It was obvious it wasn't a fit for us for a few reasons, but the main one was the bathroom. The way it was laid out meant Michael couldn't even get into the bathroom in his commode chair and have space for his caregiver to do his bowel program. Without hesitation, I simply said, "Well, this won't work, he wouldn't be able to get into the bathroom, we'd have to do his bowel program in the living room and then the entire place would smell like shit."

The young woman had a blank look on her face as she uttered an awkward, "Uhh…"

Her eyes darted to Linda and Greg. She didn't know how to respond to the shitshow. I simply said as I headed towards the door, "Well, I don't need to see the rest of the place, thanks."

The tour was immediately over, and she had no idea what I was referring to. No one gets quadriplegia unless you live with it for a bit. Even just coming around and staying for a full day would enlighten many. Just live a day in their shoes, those shoes which never touch the ground.

I had to buy Michael new tennis shoes while he was at Craig Hospital. I had to buy two sizes larger than his usual size. One of the things that can happen to a newly paralyzed person is their feet swell up. Those orange and grey tennis shoes still look brand new since they've never been used to walk, run, or touch the ground like they're supposed to. Those shoes made me sad. So much of our life was full of sadness.

Looking for a new accessible home was difficult. It was challenging to find a home to hold us with all of our many needs, now with quadriplegia taking up the space it needed. It needed its own separate room or even two. I joked around with Michael…before the accident, he was high maintenance with everything he was doing to take care of his health, but now he was even more complicated because of quadriplegia.

I was no longer able to be in denial about needing an accessible place to live, with our looming discharge date approaching on January 14th, which was only in about two weeks. I kept looking for a home. We only saw two other places and finally found one which might work.

The day after Christmas I submitted an inquiry to tour it. It was in a huge apartment complex with about 300 units. It felt like a bland corporate complex because there were many people all in their separate cubicles. They called it Amli at Flatirons. The unit was spacious, on the ground floor, and it accommodated our many needs including our bathroom ones.

After I saw it, I scrambled to secure the place by showing up the next day with my cash deposit in hand. The day after this we heard the place was ours and we were very relieved, we finally had a place to move to. This was the quickest turnaround in deciding where to live I'd ever done. It was the best Christmas gift − to find a place to hold all our needs. It could accommodate his bowel routine and house me, both Linda and Greg and their cat. They would live with us for another two months after leaving Craig Hospital to make sure we settled into our home and this new reality of living on our own with quadriplegia. This apartment was in Broomfield which was about 30 minutes from Boulder where we preferred to live. We signed a year-long lease with the hopes we'd find another accessible home to fit our personalities better.

This first apartment was what held all of us as we transitioned out of the comfort of Craig Hospital. The apartment never truly felt like our home. But to be honest I don't think any place straight out of the hospital would. We were still trying to just be at home in our new sense of ourselves and for Michael, this also meant getting to know his body in a completely different way. Well, actually, all of us had to deal with Michael's new body as all his needs were dependent on us. We became his body. I became what a mama is to their newborns − tending and caring for all of Michael's needs.

Around this time, I had two girlfriends who had just given birth and I saw many parallels to my situation. I would have to bathe and dress Michael. I would have to clean up his poop. Cleaning Michael means having to change his pants, not a diaper. It's a process that takes about an hour or more depending on how well you do at containing the mess.

I need to add here quadriplegics and paraplegics don't wear adult diapers or even underwear. They go full monty all the time to protect their skin. They sit all day on their asses, which meant if they had underwear on, it would leave an imprint on their skin leading to a pressure sore. Pressure sores are the arch-enemy of anyone with paralysis. You must be vigilant to not let it begin its ugly process. We learned about this at Craig Hospital where they showed a video of the worst outcome. The image was so utterly disgusting; I puked later that day. But the importance of skin care is ingrained in my brain because of the gruesome reality.

I also had to feed Michael, brush his teeth, and do booger patrol; Q-Tips have become my best friend. And the statement – you can pick your friends, but you can't pick your friend's nose – well, it's just not true anymore. We even bought one of those baby booger squeezers, but it didn't work very well.

We had to buy a special van to accommodate him, just like families with kids have to get bigger cars, except ours needed a special ramp to handle the wheelchair, which is essentially a very advanced "stroller." When we meet babies, they have a quizzical or all-knowing look on their faces – like, this guy is also in a baby stroller. To get out the door to go anywhere, I have to make sure I have everything I may need such as meds, extra clothing, wet wipes, gloves, and water. And my purse now has Allen wrenches in case his wheelchair needs an adjustment. It was as if I had a newborn too, except mine was 48 years old. One of my recent Mama friends made a very clear distinction though – her process was filled with the joy of caring for her newborn whereas mine was mostly full of grief.

But instead of me giving birth to a baby, this process of initiation was birthing me. I was in the process of understanding how to be a Mama to a 48-year-old newborn.

CHAPTER 11

MOVING & MIRACLES

"Home is elusive.
It shapeshifts with the currents
of my heart and its will.
Home is a trickster changing
according to the medicine
of the season and its lesson."

—Kimberly Wesnaut

Moving into this new Amli apartment happened in stages. We were all anxious about this, especially Michael. It wasn't simply a move for him, he was also beginning a life he had never imagined. A handsome, passionate guy who was always willing to help others, never dreaming he would be dependent on anyone.

Linda and Greg moved in a few weeks before the move date, and I took advantage of staying in our condo. They took the basics for what they needed and then we moved the rest a few weeks later. I enjoyed the quiet of the condo, our first and only place of cohabitation. I needed time alone which I hardly ever got.

But I wasn't really alone, I was there with Michael's able-bodied ghost. This was the place where we took the big leap of moving in together. The timing of it felt right as we'd been together for about three years. Here was the place, in my aloneness, I could process all of this; the happiness before the accident, then the grief, and the horror of it all.

There had been so many times I had prayed for solitude. I craved it, but now, alone with these walls that held the most intimate moments of our lives together, I wondered if solitude was what I needed. But, as eerie as it seemed, I breathed deep into this space of aloneness. It was a welcome interlude during this chaotic time.

We finally moved everything on January 5th, 2013, in the middle of a snowstorm with temperatures in the teens. It was brutal but we had no choice. I was grateful for our community who showed up with hats and gloves and many layers to help us. We managed to move it all in one big U-Haul truck. And our focus was getting the new place ready for Michael's arrival in just nine days!

The night before Michael's arrival I stayed with him at Craig Hospital. At 1:00 a.m. he rang the call button for me to come be with him. The call button was always placed near his head so all he had to do was slightly turn it to hit the bell. Neither of us slept that night because of the anxiety of moving him out of the hospital, the hospital had become very familiar and safe. Michael was panicking; he felt alone and full of fear. I carefully crawled into the twin medical bed with him, and he said, "I'm scared and I just need to know everything's going to be okay."

As he said this, I felt my doubts arise, but I assured him by saying, "Oh honey, I hear you...we'll get into a new routine, a new life schedule, and we'll figure it out."

He then asked me, "Do you sometimes get scared?"

"Of course I do, but we have support – Linda and Greg are staying with us through this transition and we have others too."

Then I went on to say what else was on my mind, "And I don't really believe in karma anymore because we haven't done anything to deserve this...my sense of okay-ness has been shattered – bad things can happen to anyone at any time. And I'm still waiting for this to all make some sense. I'm stuck in wondering why this happened; I'm waiting for an answer."

He sighed, and replied, "I guess we'll have to just live our way into the answer and then maybe it still won't make any sense."

This was one of the many talks we'd have in the middle of the night because one or both of us would be up with anxiety.

The move went smoothly, at least as far as I remember. I wrote nothing about this in my journal at the time. No news is good news, right? I grabbed all his belongings from his Craig hospital room along with the things I bought to make it feel more like a home, including a Norfolk Island Pine tree decorated as a Christmas tree. Once we were packed, I led the way to the new place in my tiny green car. Michael and his driver followed behind me in the disability transport van. Linda and Greg greeted us as we arrived at our first home in this next part of our life.

Our first night was quite eventful in our new apartment. There was a lot of activity happening as bringing Michael home was a huge endeavor. We had hired a home health care organization to do his morning and evening routines. They were responsible for getting Michael in and out of his chair, and in and out of bed. And then we hired another company to come and help with lunch and do other tasks like cooking, cleaning, and running errands. The nursing director and two CNAs were all standing in our open and very spacious dining/kitchen/living room when Linda suddenly lost it and started yelling, "What the fuck?!"

And then I joined in for a duet of fucks. Out of nowhere water was rapidly coming towards our feet and wheels like a mini flood on the fake wood-looking linoleum floor. Linda and I began running around in a frenzy using the word fuck about every other sentence. By now we were quite fluent in the language of rage and anger and things going very wrong.

Meanwhile, Michael was in shock but just calmly kept explaining his needs and his healthcare routine as if the flooding wasn't happening.

He later shared he was also stressed but was numb because he couldn't do anything to help us with the situation. It was the beginning of him being home with this new experience of not being able to contribute to the household in any physical way. He had loved doing his own home repairs and had quite the collection of plumbing and woodworking tools complete with a table saw! Thus more grief started to show up. We had grief upon grief upon grief; like cardboard boxes stacked on top of each other.

Linda and I were running around grabbing all the towels to stop the flow of water and figure out why this was happening. Turns out the washing machine was broken and wasn't draining properly.

A friend told me later if you don't grieve, water will show up in odd ways to remind you to get busy and do your grief work. Well, we sure had work to do! This was actually our second big water leak. A pipe had burst at the full of stairs place and we had to run fans for days. And we had to hire a company to come to make sure the moisture was all gone.

We had more chaos around this time when Greg unknowingly unplugged the upright freezer to iron his dress shirt for the Christmas gathering we had at Craig Hospital. This is a reason now for me to never get dressed up again.

Our freezer was mostly full of meat and fish. The rotten meat and fish smelled awful yet the stench was fitting for our life at the time. We were managing much more than just learning about quadriplegia. We were having to throw out many parts of our life along with months' worth of food.

Our life in this Amli apartment reminded me of the rotten fish smell but some miracles started to show up as well. One night Michael called me and our friend who was doing the overnight to come in and hear him speak. He said, "I need you two to help me with something, I'm really struggling, and I need your help to pray."

I immediately blurted out, "Pray?"

I was shocked. I knew Michael was desperate because he never prayed, nor did he ever ask for help to pray. Michael was raised both

Lutheran and Catholic (his mom was Lutheran, and his dad was Catholic) and Michael was still recovering from the latter. For as long as I have known him, he has never entered a church, nor does he ever "pray." On our trip to Spain, he even refused to enter the Cathedrals just to see the art and architecture. He'd go venturing on his own and meet up with me later. When he asked to pray, he got my full attention.

At this point I wasn't praying either, I was mad at God/Spirit for letting this happen. I used to pray by placing dear ones in God's pocket for extra protection. But apparently, that pocket had a hole in it because Michael fell through. I didn't name my lack of faith with Michael, I just pulled in closer to him and said, "Wow honey, what do you need to pray about?"

He said clearly, "I'm not sure I want to be around anymore. And if I'm going to be this miserable, it doesn't make any sense. I need a sign I'm supposed to be here."

We held space for Michael, and we all pleaded out loud to God to give him a sign. The prayer was emotional; it was short, simple, and clear; it was more like a demand. It seemed like those are the best kind of prayers, and probably easier on the Great Spirit's end as well.

The next day we got a very clear answer which was nothing short of miraculous; it felt like a direct message from God to keep living this life. The miracle came via a voicemail from a woman named Marian whose daughter had been a C-0 quadriplegic, her injury was at the base of her skull, it was at the highest level. She had been unable to breathe on her own and had relied on a ventilator 24/7. She had recently died. Marian had heard about Michael and his situation from a mutual friend. Turns out she was wondering if we needed some items to help us with our life as she no longer needed them, and her daughter had requested all her things be donated to someone in a similar situation. They were our new angels in our life; our prayers were not only heard but answered.

Michael called Marian back immediately and began to cry with a grateful heart. He told her he had asked God for a sign last night and this was his answer to keep going. We weren't just gifted chucks (absorbent pads for adults), saline, and catheters. This divine donation included all this: a Guldman ceiling lift ($12,000), a manual Hoyer lift ($2,200), an accessible van, old but in good enough condition, and most importantly, it had a lift to take Michael places in his power chair. We also got a full-sized Tempur-pedic medical bed and mattress, an FES bike ($30,000), and a standing frame ($1,999).

It was as if we had won the quadriplegic lottery. Disability is very expensive, which we were quickly learning. For example, his power wheelchair costs about $16,000!

We were quite amazed and ecstatic with this clear message; it was what Michael needed and it gave us a wave of momentum for all of us to keep going as it felt daunting to do this on our own.

Marian truly was our angel because not only did she gift us many things we needed in our new life, but she also showed up right when I needed her the most. She came one afternoon unannounced to drop off some supplies. I was gloved and ready to change Michael's suprapubic catheter. (A suprapubic catheter goes directly into his bladder. It stays in 24/7 with a small balloon filled with saline solution. The catheter is attached to a tube attached to a bladder bag where the urine collects throughout the day). One day my eight-year-old nephew, at the time, saw Michael's bladder bag filled with yellow liquid and enthusiastically exclaimed, "Oh cool, you have a constant supply of lemonade!"

Back to Marian arriving…my hands were shaking with the amount of stress I felt having to do this on my own for the first time. I was having a hard time knowing what to do, even though I'd passed the test at Craig Hospital. She knocked on the bathroom door and came in. She saw the panic in my eyes and asked if I needed any help. I graciously said yes. She said to me, "Okay watch this, I've done this a thousand times. It's quite simple."

She then calmly started giving me orders and telling me what to do. I was grateful for the support and another opportunity to learn this process from an expert. I would be this calm superpower of a presence many years later as I'd be teaching Michael's caregivers how to change his catheter. His care is really a lot and very stressful when it's all new to you.

After this, I changed his catheter once in the middle of the night and we ended up in the ER. We only had one catheter and those things are very wobbly and seem to have a life of their own. You have to be very careful not to let the part that goes into his bladder touch anything else. Well, I accidentally let it touch something and it was no longer clean. Now we know ways to disinfect it. But back then, we ended up calling the paramedics to see if they could fix it. They could not. They ended up taking us to a hospital that didn't even have the right kind of catheter he needed.

I have to explain a very important medical issue that often happens with Michael or any person with quadriplegia—Autonomic Dysreflexia (AD). It was why we ended up in the ER when we were out on our own. AD is the body's way of signaling when something is uncomfortable in the body. For example, an able-bodied person can feel that they have to pee, or they are sitting on something spikey, or they have just broken a bone. Someone with quadriplegia cannot feel this through the typical sense channels to the brain. Autonomic dysreflexia is how the paralyzed body communicates something is very wrong. When this happens to Michael, he gets a very specific headache and his blood pressure goes up. So, when he alerts me, the first thing I check is his catheter tubing. Most often it is kinked or blocked. Resolving the issue stops the symptoms immediately. Learning about this in the beginning, freaked me out, but by now, I appreciate the body's ability to send the message regardless of being unable to sense and feel what's causing it.

I also had to teach the hospital staff about AD as well as other things about caring for someone with quadriplegia. They kept giving Michael the call button, which was an actual button that you needed the ability of fingers to use it. I kept saying over and over on repeat— he can't use his fingers. I also had to ask them to have his bowel program done before they discharged him the next day. They didn't do it, I had to when we arrived back home. I was reminded that even though he was in the hospital with trained staff, they may not know much about quadriplegia. This was what it was like at the beginning at Longmont United Hospital. Yet, I was surprised I had to be the one teaching them about it and advocating for better care. I really missed the staff at Craig Hospital who knew it all.

We then began teaching our community what they needed to know in order for it to be easier and safer to be with us. We had a potluck one night and invited many friends over to learn about how to be with Michael in this new reality and specifically how to be with his chair body and what his specific needs were and how to deal with AD since we were no longer in the comfort of the hospital.

Another reason why we had it was to recruit others to help us with his overnight care. I couldn't do it every night. His sister Linda and I had been trading off every other night to cover this. Some friends volunteered and other friends did it in exchange for money. We had entered the weird territory of asking for help from our friends often and we eventually needed to pay them for this. It made sense but things start to get weird when you're paying your friends. It becomes a business transaction, and it starts to taint the friendship. It became yet another secondary loss we had to deal with.

As awkward as it was, I was grateful for the help. And it was great to see our friends and yet it was also weird. One friend pulled me aside awkwardly and whispered to me, "How am I doing?"

I replied with my voice going up to imply a question, "Uh, fine?" And she could probably see the baffled expression on my face. I do not have a very good poker face at all.

I was confused and wanted to ask her − what the hell do you mean − how're YOU doing? She then said, "I'm just nervous being around Michael and I want to do this right."

I thought—this is strange. It's not some kind of pass/fail test. He's still just Michael, his body just doesn't work like it used to. This is when I started learning not everyone could handle our situation and it really did become a test you could fail. Once again, as if our lives weren't weird enough, now we were navigating other people's hesitancy and awkwardness around all this. People don't like to be uncomfortable. But when your life is like this, there is no other option than to get cozy with discomfort.

Another dear friend told me later she was nervous to see Michael because she hadn't seen him since before the accident. But as soon as she saw him and spoke to him, she realized he was still the Michael she adored and was able to relax and enjoy him like she used to. She passed the test! And I was grateful for this.

She signed up for a few overnights and we recruited a few other volunteers that day as well. A few people came over to just hang out with us or take Michael for walks in the neighborhood. We felt grateful yet we also started feeling concerned as we started navigating our social life with the many moments of having to ask for help so often. It seems trivial and subtle, but this is huge if you're constantly asking for assistance of some kind.

Michael and I were able to share the same bedroom for part of the time in this new place. We had to share it as Linda and Greg needed the other bedroom. The master bedroom was spacious, it held both of us and we had enough room for his caregivers to comfortably do their work. We were able to set up Michael's single medical bed and my full bed frame which originally belonged to my dad's parents, Emory and Ruth. I like sleeping in a bed frame which possibly supported my father's conception.

When I was in Michael's bed, I'd have to prop myself up on the guard rails to snuggle with him. Like his wheelchair – it was uncomfortable for me. But it was something I was getting used to because I had to and being close to each other was important to us. After all, my primary love language was touch.

I was able to sleep in the same room with him in this Amli apartment and quite frankly this stunned me. I even slept through his morning routine when the CNA would come to do his stretches, feed him, then get him out of bed to do his bowel program, and then get him dressed and put him in his chair. And sometimes I'd sleep through the entire routine especially if I'd done his overnight care.

Overnight care meant I might have to get up two to four times to help him with his needs. All Michael had to do was ring the bell. He didn't sleep well, he might need a drink of water, medication to keep his blood pressure regulated or help with the blankets if he was too hot or too cold. Remember, quadriplegics cannot regulate their temperatures very well.

I would also just lay with him to help with his anxiety. Sometimes he would ring the bell by accident if he had a spasm, which was common for those with quadriplegia. One time when he rang it by mistake, he immediately apologized in his gentle middle-of-the-night voice. He later added, "You know I love you, right?"

I could never sleep in the same room with him now because of all his needs throughout the night and the fact that he needs the room to always be a balmy seventy-two degrees. I prefer sleeping cool. I was only able to do this back then with the help of prescription drugs, and at this point, I had my own bottle of Ambien. I knew one of the ways to handle this quadriplegia marathon was to get sleep anyway I could. And for me, this meant using prescription sleep aids to knock me out.

I became an expert at receiving help. I had to. There was no way of doing this on my own. And to be honest, I believe one of the reasons I survived all this was to not be afraid to ask for help and to receive it fully when it was offered. I've heard other wives or partners of those with quadriplegia, don't want anyone else taking care of their loved one. I was wired the opposite – it was easy for me to let others help us. There were times in the beginning when I'd hover and stress over how they were doing it. And I would teach and correct them as they did their jobs. But early on, I realized for me to take the best care of myself, I had to let others take care of Michael. And it's not just my job, but it's also Michael's job to ask others for help and to tell them what to do.

Yet, I still wonder how I'm able to do this to this day. One thing that helped was being able to get away completely for much-needed breaks.

CHAPTER 12

MEXICO, WALKING, AND LABYRINTHS

"The cure for anything is salt water—sweat, tears, or the sea."

—Isak Dinesen

We are tender and vulnerable inside of grief. We're like young children. If you make a promise to someone in deep grief, keep it. I'll say it again – *if you make a promise to someone in grief, keep it.* I say it twice because it still stings how many people did not keep the promises they made to me.

I remember exactly who said what and what they said they'd do. It's very interesting to me how I can remember this… "Grief-brain" is real, and many other details were hard to keep track of, but hearing how people wanted to help, it's like it was etched into my brain somehow. Many people promised to just visit us and never did. And many people said they'd take me out to dinner, and then didn't. The best gift and the one that hurt the most was when one friend wanted to gift me a short stay at an amazing hot springs resort for a long weekend. I couldn't go at the time they offered and when I finally got back to them to arrange this a few months later, it no longer worked for them. I was incredibly disappointed, and it made my heart hurt a little more.

I could have gone on my own to the hot springs, but it would have been a huge splurge and I didn't have extra cash laying around. In fact, in the first year, I was barely making enough to cover all of our expenses. I was only seeing about 5-8 clients per week compared to a full caseload of about 20-25. It was a miracle I was even able to keep my private practice going at all during that time.

Some friends and family gifted me with monthly financial support and I will be forever grateful to them. It meant I could just focus on supporting Michael and myself and the mountain of grief in front of us. I couldn't have done any of this alone. There would be no extra trip to the hot springs when I was hardly able to pay our bills. And this was why it hurt to be promised a trip to linger in healing waters, only to have it taken back.

Be mindful of what you say you'll do for a grieving person. Otherwise, you may become part of their secondary losses. Ask yourself first – why am I offering this? Is it to make myself feel better or do I truly want to help the griever possibly feel better? I've learned many people say and offer things only for the sake of making themselves feel better. They say it to feel comfortable amid an uncomfortable situation. A skill that is much needed in this culture is to be able to sit with the discomfort of life. One of my grief mentors and now blessed memory, Elder Malidoma Somé, taught me *grief is staying in the discomfort of life.* Westerners aren't good at this, and we'll do just about anything to avoid it.

We suck at sitting in discomfort – it's like wearing a wool body suit you can't take off. One of my clients described grief like this and it's a brilliant description. Being able to stay with the discomfort you feel when you're around someone whose life just got turned upside down.... well, this is the best gift of all. What we mainly need is for you to simply show up and stay around and just be with us in our pain and discomfort. Otherwise, you get put in the weird category of people who had good intentions but no follow-through, and then the address book is rearranged, and there's more grief to process.

Thankfully I was gifted a trip to Mexico in February of 2013, just six months after the accident and a few months after my promised hot springs trip. Michael's sister and her husband Greg thought I needed serious rest, so they sent me to their timeshare in Mazatlán. Armand and Bonnie came back to help while I was away because Linda and Greg also got a break too − they went to Costa Rica. We'd only been living in the apartment for about a month at the time. I used Michael's many credit card miles he'd stashed over many years to fly there. And I felt guilty for using them − he was supposed to use them for all the trips he had wanted to take.

I welcomed this trip; it was long overdue and yet it was just fucking weird. In hindsight, the timing sucked − I left on a solo trip to be in a posh resort over Valentine's Day weekend. Well, that was just stupid, but they needed to use it by a certain time, which is why I went then. And to be honest, Michael and I don't really do much for the Hallmark card holiday, but others do − especially Mexico.

I have a longtime love for Mexico. I studied abroad there in college for my junior year, which was when I was in an abusive relationship. And I lived there later in 2003 in a city called Querétaro, where I volunteered with single indigenous mothers and their children. This was through a Catholic organization called Puente de Esperanza, The Bridge of Hope. I did art therapy with the children and worked with the teen girls who came to live in the city so they could continue their education. If they stayed in the countryside where they were from, education stopped after elementary school. I enjoyed my time there. I gave my services of care and art, and they paid me with tortillas and a room in a beautiful and historic colonial building.

Mexico is where I began my reverent relationship with death by experiencing their Day of the Dead celebrations. Gathering in the graveyards where the stone arched gateway was completely covered in bright orange marigold flowers; a portal inviting you into a different place in time full of beauty and ritual. They cleaned the headstones, decorated them, and then had food and sang songs to honor and be with their beloveds, their ancestors.

Mexicans wrap their hearts around any reason to celebrate. Their holidays and festivals are full of food, loud music, singing, and dancing, and almost always end with fireworks. Valentine's Day is a special celebration too. They call it, "Dia del Amor y Amistad," Love and Friendship Day, including ALL love relationships, not just romantic ones.

However, in the realm of romance, they spared no expense. Oversized teddy bears, red heart-shaped balloons, an array of chocolates in every flavor, and roses – real or fake, for sale wherever you turned. Being in Mexico at that time intensified the sting. It felt like salt being mercilessly rubbed into an open wound, with me standing alone amidst a sea of blissful couples and joyous families. The trip was like my life – it had both equal doses of bitter and sweet.

Everything was just different about this trip – especially considering it was the first trip I took without Michael. He had a deep passion for traveling, and we had often discussed our dream destinations for future adventures. Cuba and Italy topped the list of places we longed to explore together. But here I was, without him by my side. I didn't even make it to the airport without having a grief burst. His absence hit me like a tidal wave.

As I made my way towards the terminal, grief bursts erupted again and again within me. They were sudden and overwhelming waves of sorrow triggered by my senses—moments when I would catch a glimpse, a scent, or a sound that reminded me of my profound loss. These grief bursts haunted me throughout the journey. They accompanied me during the check-in process and as I rode the underground train to the other terminal. They persisted as I stood at the gate, waiting alone. Even as I settled into my seat and peered out the window, tears streaming down my face, I couldn't help but question why I had come. "I shouldn't be taking this trip," I thought, the weight of my sorrow heavy on my heart. "If Michael hadn't fallen, I wouldn't be here... I shouldn't be here." Yet, there I sat, by the window, trapped between the conflicting emotions of longing and grief.

I was traveling alone, but I wasn't alone, this is when I started traveling with Michael's able-bodied ghost. And I'd have many moments where I'd think, oh, Michael would love this, or he would have done that. He was with me every step I took; I cried often. I also wasn't alone because *Grief* squeezed herself into my suitcase and started following me everywhere I went.

On my first day there, after settling into my room, I decided to go for a walk on the beach and eventually take a bus or cab to the huge grocery store called Mega to get my food. I was blessed with a kitchenette in my tiny space, I wouldn't have to eat out all the time and I could just stay in my private bubble, which I needed.

It was about 4:00 p.m. and I grabbed my light jacket and wallet and started walking south on the sandy beach. I thought of Michael and how nice it would be to be walking barefoot together in the warm sand. I just kept walking. I got lost in thought of what was and what now was becoming our new reality. I walked for three miles without even knowing it! Awareness had slipped into that other realm, that of how it used to be. I hadn't really been paying attention to where I was. This was very unusual for me. I had missed all the beauty, the late afternoon sun dancing across the water.

Now, pulling myself back to the present, I stopped walking to take in the beautiful sunset, flooded with awareness that the sun was setting. How could it be that late – how long had I been walking? I'd be losing the light very soon and as a solo foreign youngish woman, (I was 42), it was not the safest place for me to be walking alone on the beach. I walked towards the main street which followed the edge of the land and sea and scanned the area for a safe person to talk to. I found an older friendly Mexican man who was sweeping up trash and I asked him in Spanish where the Mega store was. He turned and pointed and told me it was right there – only a few blocks inland. I was surprised I had walked all that way. Yet it made sense because what I needed to do was begin to grok our new life; I could have walked for another two days.

I walked nearly every day on this trip, and I rested as best I could within the resort lifestyle. My room faced the main pool and every day at 10:00 a.m. they would start blaring pop music for the water aerobics class and then the music would continue until 10:00 p.m. I hated it; I'm auditorily sensitive and I prefer silence to background noise. I never did take the class, but I should have just joined in. I had mini dance parties in my room after being angry because I couldn't turn it off. If you can't beat 'em, you might as well join 'em.

A few days into my week trip, I ended up getting sick because my body was exhausted, and my immunity was very compromised. Grief lowers the immune system, it's not uncommon to become ill after a loss. And my life went from a speed of 60 mph to 0; I went from doing way too much to having nothing to do at all. I'm not surprised I began to feel sick. In fact, now I know to bring immune-boosting supplements and herbs on future trips as well as prioritize more rest and downtime in my routine to not overwhelm my body like this again.

The trip was just bizarre…being there without Michael and being in a culture that values the couple, I had many people asking me where my people were – mi marido (my husband) and niños (children). And then I'd get tears in my eyes as I explained to them in Spanish what had happened to him and us. I got good at saying "quad-dra-ple-i-a" in Spanish. That dreadful word. It sounds much better in this romance language. I wish you could hear me say it. Look it up on your smartphone and then say it out loud to yourself and notice how much better it sounds and feels as it rolls smoothly out with your lips and tongue. Is this why romance languages are called that? Because they are pleasurable to speak and sound so much better?

I'd been studying Spanish since middle school when I made the decision it would serve me far better in the future to know Spanish than German or Latin. I loved my 7th grade self – she was smart in some ways and yet she struggled in other ways, especially socially. I would say 7th grade was the worst year of my life until 2012, now I'd say they're equally horrible years for very different reasons.

I studied Spanish up into college. I have a minor in it. It helped that I'd lived there twice, so I was mostly fluent. But having to explain quadriplegia and disability in Spanish was challenging. It helped to use hand signals and gestures. Once again back to the rock, paper, scissor gestures, and using things like a hand slash across the neck to get the point across. I remember seeing the taxi driver's look of shock staring at me in the rear-view mirror as I explained once again why I was all by myself.

I rested, I slept in, I laid in the sun on my porch, and I wrote in my journal a lot. I read a lot too. I was the woman wrapped in her plush resort beach towel crying alone with my head either in a book or longingly looking out at the sea for hours. I was reading a book about soul contracts where people supposedly said yes to living awful lives even before they're born. I don't know about that for sure, but what I do know is I was trying hard to find some kind of meaning and some kind of reason as to why this happened.

My books became my travel companions and dear friends. This is when I began reading everything I could find about grief. I jokingly started referring to myself as the grief freak with "freak" meaning I was passionately obsessed with grief and my search for meaning. I even renamed my business Grief Freak for a bit. I felt like a freak because I didn't quite fit in the grief world. But this wasn't the best idea for my business, and I changed it later. We don't make the best choices when we're grieving, it's best to put off big decisions until later if we can. And I still wasn't reading about quadriplegia; I was in denial about it. And I had an unconscious thought – if I don't read about it, it's not happening.

I was the woman alone on the beach or by the pool or at the restaurant. I was reminded of the immense loneliness I experienced in

7th grade where I had no friends yet and was super shy. On Valentine's Day, I decided to treat myself to dinner at the resort restaurant. I sat at the bar perched high above the others. I thought I'd be able to have some company. I assumed there might be others alone like me wanting to eat out and be around people. And I thought at least the bartender would make conversation with me. I was mistaken, and the food wasn't great either. I left early and was disappointed and just very sad. I missed Michael as a plant misses and needs water; I was parched. I would have to find other ways of getting my needs for water met; I was determined to grow differently.

By this point in the trip, I was mostly annoyed and miserable and had wondered why the hell I had come. I had thought about going with a close girlfriend, but I realized what I needed was to just be alone. I didn't want to have to fawn to fit in, where I please others to diffuse conflict and try to re-establish safety. I didn't want to deal with that. I wanted my *Grief* to be front and center since it snuck into my suitcase anyway. It needed to be in charge because sometimes what it needed would change from minute to minute. I went alone prioritizing my needs over the need to be with someone. In some ways, this worked well, and I found my way into it. But I learned this is why people go on organized grief retreats. And, of course, I started planning to be a grief retreat director someday just like Julie, the cruise director, on the '80s TV show called *Love Boat*. Wouldn't that be cool if we had a grief boat? That's it, I could eventually be a cruise ship programs director on the grief boat!

Here's what I learned I needed after my trip – a simple companion to just be my human who was only responsible for making sure I ate, stayed hydrated, and made sure I was warm enough. And those were the only questions or suggestions they could make. If I wanted to talk to them, I could, but this wouldn't be about them at all. This person would be a grief tender. Martin Prechtel who writes about grief in his book called

The Smell of Rain on Dust states: "Take someone with you whom you trust to watch over you, someone who will not try to 'cure' you, for grief is not an illness, not something to 'get out of your system'. Bring someone who simply and solidly will assist you in only the most tangible ways: sleeping, eating, resting, staying warm, or cool as the case dictates."

On the very last night of my trip, I started to physically feel better and felt inspired to make art. I hadn't felt like making art since the accident. The only thing I'd done was to rip out a gaping hole in one page of my sketchbook, and it was so satisfying I hadn't done anything else. Plus I never had the inspiration to make more art. Grief is cruel that way. It takes away what used to soothe you.

I'm glad I packed art supplies for this trip. I almost always travel with some array of them. I brought paper, colored pencils, and charcoal. I also used the rocks I'd gathered on my beach walks and got to work. I placed these along with the paper in a line across the floor in my room, it spanned about 15 feet. I put black charcoal on the bottoms of my feet and then I walked along the paper to represent this new path we were on. I also put charcoal on my hands and placed handprints alongside the footprints to show I was crawling at times.

The next day I was sitting on the beach north of the hotel to have some privacy and not hear the blaring music. The resort set up was not helpful, and neither was the weather – it was colder than usual. For many reasons, this trip was challenging for me. The colder weather meant the ocean wasn't very warm, I wasn't swimming in it as much as I had hoped I would. I much preferred to swim in the ocean vs the chlorinated pool near the awful loud music.

I was sitting on the beach, my feet and hands in the sand, and started placing the large ocean-smoothed rocks near me into a pile and began drawing lines in the sand around them. And suddenly like a lightning bolt, I knew what I needed to do. I had to create a labyrinth! A labyrinth is a circular path that leads you to the center. It looks like a maze but it is not, because you follow one solid path to the center and then turn around and follow the same path out. A labyrinth would mirror my upside-down reality—this mysterious and meandering path I found myself on, walking to the center and back out, but not easily. No, I had to walk with all its twists and turns, going in one direction and then finding myself in a complete 180-degree turn. The labyrinth would help bring peace around all that we'd lost yet it would also beautifully nudge me towards embracing whatever lay ahead. The maze-like path would help me surrender and trust the wisdom that guided us. I would become one of the thousands who for centuries have used these complicated paths to delve into one's depths, uncover hidden truths, and ultimately discover the profound beauty that lies at the core of our being.

I attempted to draw this from my memory but struggled to get it right. Labyrinths are complicated, ever draw one without a diagram? Me neither. Their designs range from a simple spiral to others with very complex patterns, with the most famous labyrinth inside the Chartres Cathedral in France.

I ran back to my room in a creative frenzy grabbing supplies – water, sunscreen, the rocks I'd collected on my walks and brought back to my room to sleep with, my journal, and what felt most important – the black charcoal. I put on my bikini under my clothes knowing at some point I would brave the cold ocean and jump in. And then I went to the internet room and managed to make a tiny printout from the Chartres Cathedral. Once I had my diagram for healing, I ran back to the beach. It felt very good to have a purpose and direction. I felt inspired for the first time since the accident. And this was the fastest I had moved my body in six months! I felt good.

Now, back where I started, I easily created a perfectly drawn labyrinth. It was huge – it must have been about 25-30 feet in diameter. I was impressed I was able to do this. With the labyrinth in place, I then grabbed my charcoal and the rocks I had collected, and I wrote the things I needed to let go of on them. I wrote – *Michael's able-body, able-bodied sex, hiking, walks, holding hands, getting pregnant*, and as thoughts took me deeper, I wrote more. Then I placed these in the middle of the labyrinth stacked in a precarious cairn, a rock tower. I felt satisfied, content, sad, tired, and proud.

A man walked by and gave me a small branch from a bougainvillea bush. I placed the bright pink, magenta flowers in the middle of the labyrinth next to the rocks. With the addition of something alive, blooming, and full of color my piece felt complete.

Some people I met the night prior saw what I was doing from their hotel balcony and came with curiosity to see my creation. When I explained it, they asked if they could walk it. I enthusiastically said yes! How I wished we had met at the beginning of my trip. Why is life always like this? You finally find what you need and then it's time to go.

Another person came along with her curiosity, and she said to me, "I figured this had to have special meaning because you were spending a lot of time with this. I just had to come and see what you were doing, and I need to know why?"

I shared my story with her. She listened intently and then asked if she could hug me. And of course, I said yes. It felt good to receive this love and connection after craving it all week.

After my newfound friends left, I sat down against an eroded sandbank and waited. I felt very proud to have created something of such beauty and I was impressed with how well it turned out. I drew it with my hands and had to crouch down to do this. It was like I had created my own mini workout like the hotel water aerobics class – sign up now for labyrinth lunges! My legs were very sore the next day, but it was worth it. I enjoyed this kind of pain; it reminded me of my creativity coming through and that I had used my able body to do it.

While I was making the labyrinth, I realized this was the reason why I was sent on this miserable trip to Mexico by myself. I had to begin my healing journey with this labyrinth and mini grief ritual with the ocean and these strangers as my witnesses. And I started a new-found relationship with walking long distances.

By this time, it was late afternoon, and I was both getting hungry and cold and the tide was coming in. The waves were getting closer to the middle of the labyrinth, I had decided to stay until the waves knocked over the cairn of stones. It was only then I'd feel complete.

I waited and after about an hour I was beginning to feel impatient. I decided to move the rocks closer to where the waves were coming from. And just when I was about to do this, one wave came and kissed my feet. It was as if it was saying, "No, no Beth, you must wait, you cannot rush this, you cannot rush your grief – it has its own pacing, its own time."

So, I put on my jacket and wrapped my legs and feet in my towel and sat back against the sand, and watched. Twenty minutes later it happened in one split second— the wave came in and the tower of stones fell instantly. I immediately thought of Michael's crash and how his neck also broke in one tiny instant. This one moment in time turned our entire life upside down. I sat there in reverence, relief, immense sadness, and a strange sense of awe. I was instantly reminded of how precious and fragile life is and how fragile we all are. I sat there with relief as more tears flowed.

I then went into the ocean for a bit even though the water was fucking cold. I wanted to finish this ritual with the ocean cleansing me and wiping off the grief I was carrying.

I believe the best grief therapist is the ocean. As Isak Dinesen says, "The cure for anything is salt water—sweat, tears, or the sea." I managed to combine all three in this one spontaneous ritual.

At this point, I was a mess even though I had immersed my body in the ocean. I was covered in charcoal simply from making the art and I'd also started drawing on myself as well. I had to throw out my cute orange, pink, white, and brown striped bikini – the blackness from the charcoal just wouldn't wash out, just like I couldn't wash it away from my own life either. But I didn't throw Michael away. And I didn't throw our life away either.

The next day I woke up early to go back to the labyrinth and see what happened overnight and then I had to pack to leave to fly back to Colorado. When I arrived at the site, the labyrinth was gone, which was no surprise because of the tide. All the stones with my writing of my losses were also gone. It pleased me to know the ocean had pulled them in and they were being washed off, just like it was still cleaning out my internal soot of grief. The only thing that remained on the beach was the small branch of bright magenta bougainvillea flowers! It made me cry with joy to see them, they became a symbol of hope for me, the beauty was still there after the tide had come and gone. I was delighted and content. It was as if the Universe or great Spirit was giving me a message to keep going, to keep walking, to continue grieving, making art and ritual, and to keep going on this healing path. I was ready to fly home and enter back into my upside-down life knowing I was slowly on this journey of coming right side up.

CHAPTER 13

MOBE

*"The universe is an example of love. Like a tree. Like the ocean.
Like my body. Like my wheelchair. I see the love."*

—Ram Dass

Arriving home after my trip to Mexico was bizarre and bittersweet,
just like my entire trip had been. I was happy to be with Michael
again, yet I wasn't quite used to the way my home had become his
medical hub, which made sense because he needed a lot of care and
attention. Walking through the front door into the apartment was
strange, it was like I had to leave my needs at the door; Michael's needs
were the priority now.

My life became a big 'both/and' or an 'on the one hand/on the
other hand' experience. It reminds me of Playback Theatre which
Michael and I love. The actors ask for stories from the audience and
then they spontaneously play it back for you through their creative
interpretations. One of their warmups is called "On the one hand,"
where they take two contrasting ideas where you hold both experiences
at the same time. It would be interesting for me to have this part of my

life played back. On the one hand, I was happy to arrive home and be with my love again, yet on the other hand, I was frustrated to return to caregivers coming and going throughout the day. My home had become a place of employment for all these home healthcare aids. I was happy to have them there because otherwise I'd have to do it all, yet on the other hand it was too much. I was realizing not only had I lost my able-bodied partner but also my sense of privacy and ultimately what home used to be for me.

Another both/and experience was his power wheelchair. I need to introduce you to it here. We call it Mobe, pronounced Mo-bee, M for Michael, B for Beth, Mo for mobility, and Be for just being with it all. This name came much later, like five years later. And by now we have Mobe One, and Mobe Two as they only last about eight years.

I have a love/hate relationship with Mobe. It's like Michael's shell and his body is the mushy snail. It's sad but very true. This shell is now part of his body, his new identity, and his sense of home. It's a place for his body to get around in and interact with the world.

I love it for this reason— it makes the world mostly accessible, yet I hate the fact that we need it. It allows Michael to move around in the world but on the other hand, it's very inaccessible in a world that is able-bodied centric. I was keenly aware of how challenging the world is because we were now trying to navigate it with wheels. So much of the world is not accessible, especially hiking trails.

Before the accident, Michael was the one who'd go off-trail when we were hiking, and I'd stay on the trail, like a typical Virgo, and follow the guidelines and care for the land this way. But not Michael – he'd go where his heart and curiosity led him. I once followed him up the side of a mountain in the Poudre Canyon near Fort Collins.

One day early on in the Amli apartment, we were outside, and he decided to just go off the sidewalk into an innocent area of small landscaping rocks and immediately got stuck. And I had to try to get him out. His wheels just kept spinning, digging himself deeper into the earth. I tried putting down cardboard to free his wheels, but doing this only made it worse. I had to ask a young man who was walking by to help us. This is when we started making friends with any bystanders as I would often need help in certain situations, especially with Mobe. I had to ask for help. His chair would get stuck when he wasn't on a sidewalk or smooth surface. These are now off limits – dirt trails, small pebbles, and the worst is sand. We also get stuck with throw rugs and sometimes even carpets. Those are all off-limits now.

I've had to bond with his wheelchair the hard way, it's mostly made of metal after all. At Craig Hospital I ran over my toes once while putting it away for the night after I put Michael in bed. That hurt, but luckily, I didn't break anything—I was wearing my bright red crocks which also survived. The chair itself weighs 350 pounds, then add Michael's weight of 150 pounds for a total of 500 pounds! After this incident, my feet had an intuitive sense to move out of the way quickly, like I had eyeballs at the tips of my toes. I've also accidentally bumped into Mobe many times and given myself bruises. It beats me up for sure!

I wish they would consider making the chairs more "user friendly," although the chair is made for the person needing to use it. But I wish they'd consider his caregivers who also have to deal with it. I wish it was made out of softer materials too, something easier to hug and interact with, like a plush recliner. That'd be nice.

It does have a special gel seat cushion. Since he sits on his ass all day long, the seat is designed to allow his sit bones to settle into an area that isn't as hard as the rest. This is also why you'll see him doing a 'tilt back'. A tilt-back is when his chair leans all the way back so the blood in his buttocks can move to prevent pressure sores. He has to do this many times a day to prevent any skin sores from developing.

Over the years I've learned how to connect to Michael's 'chair body' better. I've learned how to cuddle with metal and wheels. And we now have daily times of connecting physically where I'll sit on Michael's lap either facing towards him or have my back against his chest facing outwards. Once while sitting outside, I was facing him with my legs straddled on either side. We were just enjoying the moment embracing each other and our friend took a photo of us and posted it on Facebook. Someone commented, "Geez you two…get a room!"

This was amusing at first but then it was not funny at all. Even though it was said lovingly, it brought up a lot of grief. Yes, I'd love to rent a room but what he's implying about taking some private time for sex would mean I'd also have to hire someone to help me get Michael in position, and then I'd have to inject his penis with medicine to make it erect.

CHAPTER 14

SEX

"It's just human. We all have the jungle inside of us.
We all have wants and needs and desires, strange as they may seem.
If you stop to think about it, we're pretty creative,
cooking up all these fantasies. It's like a kind of poetry."

—Diane Frolov
and Andrew Schneider

Sex. I have to talk about it. I thought I'd start an entirely new chapter addressing this subject. Sex needs an entire chapter, and perhaps it's my next book. In general, we don't talk about sex enough and then hardly at all regarding disability. And we need to and when you add grief to the mix, we talk about it even less.

At Craig Hospital we were given a guidebook about taking care of yourself while providing care. It only devotes about three pages to the complexity of sexuality after a spinal cord injury. They also gave me a booklet entitled. "PleasureABLE: Sexual Device Manual for Persons with Disabilities" which was much more useful and direct in its approach.

Yet, I wouldn't look at these until later because my grief about it was too overwhelming.

Our able-bodied sex life as we knew it, was dead. And in the beginning, I was confused, and my body was too. My body craved Michael's body and his touch. I would wake up crying for the first three weeks. My body felt lost without his body. My vagina strongly felt the absence of his erect penis. He was no longer able to have a natural and normal erection and for many years after the accident activating anything related to sex also came with huge amounts of grief for me. I admit I avoided being sexual with him.

It was too hard for me to feel this kind of loss; the amount of grief was huge. And it was the biggest secondary loss for me. Sex was bittersweet and for the first few years, I had too much sadness regarding our able-bodied sex life, it was really hard for me to talk about and even harder to do.

Before the accident, we had been diving deep into our intimate and sexual connection. I had just been experiencing orgasms unlike I'd ever had or ever dreamt were possible. I was making huge strides in my ability and capacity to be sexual. Michael was the best lover I ever had. He had been patiently teaching me to relax and to drop into sensation more. As a result, I could feel my orgasms through my entire body and out through my fingers and toes! We were both excited to continue expanding this part of our relationship. To suddenly lose this deeper exploration of our sexuality was incredibly painful. I would say it has been my deepest grief.

I've finally said what you've all been probably wondering about – sex. Two things we don't talk about openly much in this culture – sex and grief; both are taboo. And unfortunately for me, sex now comes with grief, so it's a double whammy.

I even had a few random strangers ask me if Michael's penis worked! I was appalled at these questions, but then because I had fierce honesty as my superpower, I would ask them about their sex lives and ask about their partner's genitals too. I learned a lot of people are actually very dissatisfied with their sex lives for many reasons. And we would bond over this. Another unexpected gift of this accident is I've become much more open about my sexuality. I'm now sex-positive, which is seeing sexuality as a normal human need and expression and there's no reason to be ashamed about it.

A few years after the accident, I was having dinner at a restaurant with a close girlfriend, and I was openly speaking about my vagina and orgasms. She leaned towards me across the tiny table for two and shushed me and told me to keep my voice down. And I replied, "I will not keep my voice down. We're all sexual human beings, and we need to talk about it openly."

Okay, I did lower my voice a bit to be mindful of her request and I also glanced around to see if any young kids were there listening. But to be honest, I want to live in a world where one can speak freely about sex as well as grief. It's such a gift to be able to experience sexual pleasure with myself or my partner or someone else.

At the beginning of our disabled life, we had to get creative with sex since the normal ways of being sexual were compromised. The answer to whether or not his penis worked was no, it didn't work in the usual able-bodied way. His penis could get an erection but only randomly when something would brush against it like a hand, his blanket, or his clothes. It made for embarrassing and awkward moments with a few caregivers. We'd explain his erection wasn't personal, and for me, this would just bring more grief. I could no longer make his penis erect like I used to.

No, now we'd need an injection of medication to hold an erection. I'd have to carefully stick a needle into his penis in the right place, I had to be extra cautious about not putting it into any veins or arteries. At first, I had our caregivers inject him as it was hard for me to put on my 'nurse's hat to prep him for sexual activity. Sticking a needle in his penis isn't exactly my idea of foreplay; it definitely kills the mood!

Gone are the days of spontaneity, which is one of the things I loved most about easy able-bodied sex. The injection would take thirty minutes to show results if we got it right. Then I'd have to do all the work to get us both in position. I was inspired to get more limber and physically fit because this was a workout. And it was hard to simply receive when you are the one on top all the time.

And to be honest, I really wasn't able to be fully sexual in the first year or two. It was hard on Michael (no pun intended) as he wanted me to be on board and on top, but for me being sexual came with grief. Not to mention grief has a huge impact on one's libido – it lowers it tremendously. I was managing both my grief and my waning libido at the same time.

We had to get creative and practical with our lovemaking. We did have one sexual highlight in the Amli place which occurred following an orgasm when my body started shaking. I had been standing on pillows and a footstool on our couch with my hands holding me in place against the wall. It was precarious and it was as if I had another superpower of receiving his pleasure while also making sure I didn't fall over at the same time! In this position, Michael was then able to do a tilt-back in his chair so he could go down on me. Even just writing about this position was hard to describe, imagine actually doing it! And I'm telling you all this because I'm sex-positive and I talk about sex openly now. If you're feeling uncomfortable about this, I invite you to just be curious about what's coming up for you. We're all sexual beings to some extent so let's embrace it and enjoy it while we can, especially while it's easy for you and your partners. I will never take sex for granted again.

Now, after that orgasm, I started having subtle shaking movements all over my body. You could see the tiny micro-movements – my body was completely releasing what it needed to—the accumulation of the trauma and grief which seemed to be stored deep within. Michael and I both knew what was happening and he encouraged me to just relax fully and let it sequence out. Later I discovered this is an actual practice called TRE-tension or trauma release exercises. And I found a training on it locally and signed up to learn more about it. (See the listing of this as a resource in the back of the book). I needed to learn more about how my body was reacting to the jumbled collection of stress and grief.

One of the things that's so amazing about being able-bodied is you can sense someone else and feel them sensing and feeling you. Now when I touch Michael where he's paralyzed, which is everywhere below his nipples, and in his arms starting at mid-forearm he starts to have sketchy sensations down to nothing in his fingers. He cannot fully feel me touching him. He cannot receive my touch, and he cannot give back in this way either. Taking in touch is also giving it back to the one who's giving it. It's an exchange of physical touch, sensation, and energy. And for him, most of his body is now an altered channel. And to me in the beginning this was very unsatisfying. We had so much to learn and so much grief to process.

Eventually, we did learn how to drop into a new relationship with our sexuality and would come to explore connecting energetically. The largest sex organ is actually the brain, and we began to use our imaginations to connect. We also just made time for what we called 'skin to skin' or 'connect time.' This involved getting into bed together – I would either get him out of his chair and into bed or his caregiver would. And then we would just lay naked and settle into each other's presence for a bit. Sometimes this would lead to being sexual but most of the time we would fall asleep together. Even this to me felt satisfying, which was very different from before because eventually, we would no longer sleep in the same bedroom. We slept separately because of all his extra needs in the middle of the night. Yet another loss.

Because of all our limitations with our sexuality, we were forced to expand our repertoire of what sex actually is and with whom. Sex could be laying skin to skin and going in and out of sleep together. Sex could be me in his wheelchair straddling him and connecting energetically. Our experience of contact improvisation was helpful here. We could linger in the pleasure of simply rubbing our faces together slowly. However, it was incredibly different than where we were sexually before the accident.

I learned to adjust, but it was hard. My friend Victor Warring, a sex and relationship coach, said I was navigating both grief and desire at the same time which was hard to do. This was also really hard for Michael as well. So, we did what we could and got creative. We communicated a lot and had some hard conversations too. I admitted to him it was hard for me to be sexual when it brought up so much grief. You cannot be in grief and be fully dropped into your sexuality, those two just don't go well together. They're like oil and water. Grief takes all the energy from sexuality. This is sad because sexuality has healing potential during grief if one can access it. We must find ways of accessing pleasure when we're grieving.

We found other ways to open the pleasure channels. For Michael, this meant discovering new places to feel orgasmic energy. One of the beautiful things about a body with quadriplegia is the place of orgasm migrates elsewhere, it's not totally lost. One just has to be open and determined to find it. We took our time and enjoyed this process, but it wasn't the same.

My grief about our able-bodied sexuality also threw me into very new territory – the idea of being polyamorous to get my physical needs met. I remember a friend asking me during the first few days after Michael's accident, "Beth, what are you going to do about your sex life?"

I surprisingly said to her, "Maybe we'll have to have an open relationship."

This was something I had never thought about before this, I had always been monogamous. And it was also something Michael and I had never discussed; we made an assumption we were monogamous.

An odd thing began to happen with my male relationships at this time—a few alluded to meeting my sexual needs but it was never straightforward like this— Hi Beth, if you need to have sex with me to satisfy your physical urge, I'm available.

No, they were often sideways. I wouldn't understand until a few hours later when I'd finally get it and my eyes would open wide in full comprehension. I wished they could have been direct and if we lived in a sex-positive culture they could've, and it would've been much easier. And now I wonder—did they ask Michael about this first? Did they even think about asking Michael if they could offer me their 'friends with benefits' benefits?

A few years later, after feeling the grief I was holding about ablebodied sex, I asked Michael to allow us to explore an open relationship. This was really hard for me to do. It took a year for me to build up the courage to ask for this. And when I finally did, it was incredibly difficult for Michael to hear. The need to satisfy my physical and sexual needs almost cost me my entire relationship with him. If I could go back and do it all over again differently I would. I was naive and very inexperienced, and I made a few mistakes along the way.

I allude to it here briefly because it's an important part of our story. On the one hand, I was proud I advocated for my sexual needs, yet on the other hand I could have done it in a better way. This may be the topic of my next memoir. We're still in the process of picking up the pieces from the rupture this created and the story isn't ready to be told.

I bring it up here because it deserves way more attention, especially in a culture that doesn't embrace sexuality fully and is mainly monogamy oriented. My dear reader, if you're in a conundrum about getting your sexual needs met, sometimes the best thing to do is the scariest thing you have to do. There are options, just do it with compassion, full understanding, and one hundred percent consent. Your sexual needs matter.

While living at the Amli apartment I began to drop deeper into my sexual grief. When we first arrived there, my sex life felt empty and devoid of life, like the apartment which seemed to be a modern ghost town. It was a colossal place built for hundreds of people, yet I hardly ever saw anyone there. However, I would often hear my neighbors having sex. I would lie awake listening to them, eyes teary and heart heavy, I would let out a sigh and quietly mumble to them unknowingly through the thin walls– bless you two, enjoy it. I really missed having able-bodied sex.

CHAPTER 15

MORE MOVING, MORE MIRACLES

"I have arrived, I am home."

—Thich Nhat Hanh

Amli Apartments – Our two-bedroom, two-bath apartment came with all the bells and whistles including its own unique smell called "blue denim" which was in an automatic timed dispenser in the hallways. What is it about having a signature smell? Do people get excited about this kind of artificiality? One day a dear friend hugged me and said, "Oh, you smell like your apartment building."

I hated smelling like blue denim; we went rogue after that and took out the batteries of the device which was right outside our door. This smell was not us and the place wasn't us at all either. But we desperately needed something, and it HAD to be accessible. It was another example of the bittersweetness of our life – we were both grateful and annoyed; we hated it yet needed it.

And we knew this was only a transitional place for us. Back in November of 2012, I received an email from a friend of ours who we met through our training with Annie Brook. She's an older woman in her 60s who is now a spiritual director. The email was short but the attachment she sent was long but very welcome. It was regarding an affordable home being built in a new neighborhood in our ideal location – Boulder, Colorado. It would be north of the city and very close to the foothills with access to many trails and open space.

We were super excited because they were building what we had been looking for — an accessible home! This was part of the Boulder Affordable Housing Program and you had to enter the lottery to get in. The deadline for this was within one week. I immediately shifted my focus at the time and did everything I needed to do to make this possible. I felt like a superwoman powered by my love for Michael. I had laser focus to get a massive amount of paperwork to them just to enter this housing contest.

Exhausted and relieved after we got on the list, we were elated to be in the queue. This high was quickly followed by a low when we learned that to qualify for the affordable housing program, I'd have to sell the beautiful condo I owned in Denver. I was devastated and angry. Why couldn't life just give us some ease, please? Once again, I was yelling at God to lighten up.

I loved my condo. It was part of a four-plex built in the 1950s and its cuteness came with coved ceilings and arched doorways. I painted it my favorite colors—blue, aqua, turquoise, yellow, and orange. The bedroom was Frida Kahlo cobalt blue – I'd taken a photo of her blue house in Coyoacàn, Mexico when I was there and brought this in to match the color at the paint store. I loved this room; it felt like you were underwater. The kitchen was a pale yet bright yellowish-orange, and the living room was a light green-blue turquoise, like copper patina. The colors made it feel like you should be in Florida, not in the middle of metro Denver.

I renovated the kitchen with what I call disco ball granite — it was black with flecks of mirrors that glimmered brightly. It gave me a lot of joy. I left the original white wooden cabinets intact. I loved their practicality —they went all the way up to the ceiling, instead of leaving the gap at the top that just collects dust because who takes the time to clean it?

More grief started to show as I came to grips with letting go of yet another thing I loved. The condo reminded me of our early dating days when Michael would drive up in his car and shlep all his stuff up the stairs. If I'd known what was to befall us years later, I would have savored those simple life moments more. It was hard to let go of this; it reminded me of a much simpler time in my life.

I didn't really have the bandwidth to deal with putting it on the market. But I didn't have a choice and immediately put it up for sale because I only had a few months to sell it, otherwise, I wouldn't be able to buy the accessible home that we desperately needed.

It was another both/and experience...on the one hand, I didn't want to sell this beautiful place yet on the other hand I was completely happy to let go of my role as a landlady. The tenant at the time was calling the plumber to unclog her toilet! Had no one ever shown her what a plunger was for?

Within a few weeks, I had a cash offer. I was super excited and relieved, and I was ready to make the deal. Then I ran into more roadblocks – the buyer had one pet too many and this violated the HOA bylaws. Fuck HOA bylaws, whoever reads those anyways? Obviously, I hadn't. I was livid and utterly disappointed, again. I learned about this while driving, I had to pull over and calm down—the dragon was wide awake again.

It's stressful to sell a home, but when you have a deadline to meet, it makes it almost unbearable. I ended up hiring another lawyer who helped me change the bylaws and deal with my rigid condo mates so I could sell my place to someone who had one dog and two cats.

I was angry because I felt like no one had compassion and empathy for my situation. Did they not know what quadriplegia meant? I was learning many people don't. I became very self-centered. I didn't care who bought the unit, I had to sell it. Therefore, I did everything I could in my power to change the HOA regulations for someone having more than two pets. I would have let a zoo live there as long as I could sell the place.

I already had enough happening and then you add the stress of putting my house on the market and having to hire a lawyer to sell it. This, on top of the already stressed-out pile of shit that was my life— dealing with Michael's medical situation, living inside hospitals, looking for an accessible transitional home, and navigating Michael's family dynamics.

It was just too much.

I managed to sell my place which was a bittersweet moment. But if selling my condo meant Michael and I had a chance to get into an accessible home in Boulder, I would do it. There was no hesitation. Later we learned because of Michael's disability we didn't even have to enter the lottery — they simply put us in one of the two accessible units. This was a huge relief.

This became official in November of 2012 when we were still trying to find the first place which would house us after he left Craig Hospital—the strange slightly artificial conglomerate of a place called Amli at Flatirons. It never quite felt like home. It was what held us as we transitioned through the liminal quadriplegic goo while our other home was being built.

Home brought many difficulties and challenges but eventually gave me lessons and helped me to stand up for both of us with what we needed. One of the benefits of this whole ordeal was I began to step up and into my power. Michael could see it too and was very proud of me. It all began with a situation with his family when his oldest sister Julie arrived on the scene.

It happened around 9 p.m. in mid-September of 2012, toward the beginning when Michael was in the ICU for 45 days. My friend Merryl came over to read me a bedtime story, rub my back and tuck me into bed early. Just as she was about to say goodbye, we heard arguing down below. The family room was right beneath my bedroom, and I could hear Michael's dad and his sister Julie yelling at each other.

My nervous system was immediately on guard and all Merryl had done for my body went out the door, just like I would a few minutes later. We both got up and out of bed and quietly went to the top of the stairs to hear what the kerfuffle was all about. Merryl pulled me in close and whispered to me, "Beth, this is your house, you don't have to put up with this."

And my brain caught up to what she said and I heard my inner voice say — oh, right! I said goodbye to Merryl as she smartly snuck out of the conflict zone. I then took a deep breath and went down the stairs. I knew exactly what I wanted to say so without hesitation I said loudly yet calmly, "This is my house and I do not want this kind of energy here. We need to focus on Michael's healing, not argue with each other! This is not okay!"

We had all been under incredible amounts of stress and things were beginning to go slightly sideways. Julie and Armand were clearly upset, and my words put her over the edge. She began yelling at me and coming towards me as well. Her words were like daggers, yet I don't remember what she said. For the first time, my body was preparing to hit someone—my inner dragon was ready to spit fire. Instead of doing something I knew I'd regret, I turned away from her as quickly as I could and ran up the half flight of stairs, and opened the screen door with my closed fists. I hit the door instead of my sister-in-law. I ran out into the night in my bare feet and pajamas and bolted for my little green car tucked into our garage.

Once inside I fell apart and began to sob. I cried out, "Okay Universe this is fucked up. I really miss Michael. I miss our old life. I miss our home. This is just awful. I can't even live in peace in my own house! Help me please, show some ease, just send me some fucking ease please."

A few minutes later there was a tap at the passenger window. It was Linda, Michael's other sister, who joined me in the car. We hugged each other and cried. And then we talked about all things related to Michael and I got the crash course of the family dynamics, especially now because Julie had arrived on the scene.

Turns out Julie left and booked herself into a hotel, which seemed to be better for all of us. We didn't have room to host her; she was just sleeping on our couch in the living room. She also seemed to have misunderstood me and thought I didn't want her in my house. I simply didn't want anyone acting like an asshole in my house when Michael was fighting for his life in the ICU.

I told Michael the next day and he was very proud of me for standing up for him and for myself. I was proud of myself too. I was finding my potency, which is the gift anger can bring if you can find a way to connect with it. Anger is a strong energy, and it teaches us to act when our boundaries have been crossed. I began to walk stronger when Michael couldn't walk at all.

One of our hardest moments living in the Amli place was the day Linda, Greg, and Willow left us to return to their normal lives. We had been preparing for this day, but we wouldn't know what it'd be like to be completely on our own until they were gone.

They left on March 15th, the Ides of March. Julius Caesar was assassinated on this day, and it is now considered a day of bad luck. Interestingly it was also known as the beginning of the year in the northern hemisphere because spring begins around then with the first shoots peeking through the soil. It felt like a mix of both for us – it was bad luck they were leaving AND it was the beginning of our life completely on our own with the newest member of the family – quadriplegia.

I had gotten used to them being a part of our community. I leaned on Linda quite often emotionally and she was my partner in crime with all things related to Michael and quadriplegia. She and Greg were also amazing cooks, and I would arrive home to the smell of home-cooked meals wafting in the hallway. Reminds me how cooking is what really makes a house a home.

The day of their departure was a beautiful spring day. They had all their stuff packed in their little red Prius. We hugged goodbye with strong embraces held longer than usual. I was trying to just hold on a moment longer, trying to squeeze out more of their support, as if their hugs could infuse the strength to do this on my own. I could feel the heaviness of all the responsibility on just me now.

Michael and I cried as they drove away. I turned to him, and we hugged each other as we wept together. He then looked at me lovingly with tears in his eyes and said, "Beth, I want you to know I'm going do everything I can to make sure this is not all on you. I'll find help. We can do this."

I felt grateful to him for saying this; knowing I truly couldn't do all this on my own. And it took us working together to figure this out. One of my many jobs was to allow others to care for him, otherwise, I wouldn't be able to have a career or any semblance of a personal life at all.

And just as our lovely north Boulder home was being built near the foothills of the Rockies, we too were building this new life together one day at a time. We were beginning to grok all our losses and learn how to deal with Michael's limitations. He was like a newborn except much bigger and heavier and not as soft nor as easy to care for as an infant. We were both struggling with our new life, but we were doing what we had to do to feel comfortable in our new homes and identities.

Our new little permanent home was perfect for us. Just shy of 1500 square feet, with three bedrooms—one for Michael, one for me, and one for the overnight caregivers. It has two levels with my space in the basement. I call my space the "woman's womb" as if you're saying woman's room with a lisp. Along with a bedroom, there is another bathroom with a bathtub and a small open space at the bottom of the stairs which would later become my office space during the pandemic.

It would also become my creative healing space or as one friend described it— the shaman's cave.

I needed a place separate from the upstairs so I could get away from the caregivers when I needed a break. Again, so grateful for them, for without them I would have to do all his care. But on the other hand, it was as if we were living with about ten different roommates all with quirky ways of doing things. Apparently, I have loads of patience.

We are blessed to live near the foothills where the trails and trees and the spring creek would become my dear friends. I would *companion* these beings. Or they would *companion* me. Our house is the wildest one in the neighborhood with raised garden beds taking over our entire small but existent front yard. And the backyard looks out onto the community's open space and the bike path.

We moved in during another snowstorm in early December of 2013. And we did this again with help from our community. By this time, I had become a metal music fan. I was listening to AC/DC, Metallica, and Rage Against the Machine as their songs soothed the dragon within me. It's how I began to deal with my rage. It was pure perfection when the song *Highway to Hell* came on the radio as I pulled out of the Amli parking lot in the rented U-Haul. I cranked up the volume and began to sing and cry as I drove west towards the mountains, towards home. Spirit was with me again, this time as the DJ. Ever notice how this happens when you really need it?

I drove up to our new home and was greeted by our community who were there to help us unpack all our stuff and get things set up for Michael's care. The windows were steamy from all the love in the small amount of square footage.

We had finally arrived home. Now we could settle in on the land that would hold us and begin the next stage of our healing journey. As we unpacked our boxes we could also begin to unpack and process all the grief that had been piling up since August of 2012.

We would come to learn that not only did we win the lottery of this new accessible home in Boulder, but it also came with amazing neighbors beyond just borrowing an egg or cup of flour. I had never lived in a neighborhood where it truly felt like a village. And this is what we got as many of our neighbors would help us out often and would become good friends too. Many had young children and I got to nurture these relationships and become the weird yet cool 'auntie' to them. This would be a balm to my moments of childless grief that would randomly rear its ugly head.

Shortly after we moved in there was a huge snowstorm and we heard a knock at the door. I thought to myself—who's knocking at this time of night in this storm? It was the twelve-year-old neighbor from down the street. He was dressed in many layers and holding a shovel with a beaming smile. He blurted out, "Hi, I'm here to shovel your walk."

I said, "Okay that's great, how much will it be?"

He quickly replied, "My mom says for you it's free."

Apparently, the word got out that a quadriplegic man and his partner had moved in. I was so grateful for the help. And was feeling so much more at home with these compassionate and interactive neighbors.

CHAPTER 16

FINDING SOBONFU SOMÉ & THE DAGARA GRIEF RITUAL

"Have you grieved enough?"

—Sobonfu Somé

Big grief needs a big container. My grief felt huge and heavy, and I was still dealing with it. I needed to find ways to be with it. Francis Weller, grief psychotherapist and my grief mentor says, "Grief requires two things to be moved – one is containment and the other is release. If I'm doing it privately, I'm asked to do two jobs at once, which I cannot do, I end up becoming an ongoing vessel for grief, but I'm never really allowed to set it down."

I learned of Weller's work in 2016 when Merryl gifted me his book, *The Wild Edge of Sorrow* for my birthday. I highly recommend it if you are broken open by grief as I was. I needed to gather up all the parts in one place and then and only then could I begin to release it.

The water leaks were perhaps a sign from Spirit that it was time to grieve. Water's main gift is about flow. If our grief could flow like water, well, we wouldn't get stuck in grief. We especially get stuck in grief in our Western culture because we have no fucking clue how to grieve. And I had to learn how to live with this amount of grief because it would be with me every day. I had to find out-of-the-box ways of moving it and I also needed to find others who I could learn from who were also stained by grief.

Stained by grief—after the accident I wanted to dye a black streak in my hair, eventually I did a streak of hot pink. I wanted to mark myself somehow, like in the old days when a widow would wear black for a year or in the Jewish tradition where they rip one's clothing to mark the mourning. I wanted the outside world to know my insides were upside down. Grief feels like you've been eaten, chewed up, and digested by a vulture. And then you come out the other end eventually. It's a shitty journey—being in the bowels of grief. It's an inside job and you must do the work to find your true north and come right side up again.

I had the pleasure of meeting a wonderful, wise woman named Sobonfu Somé in person in 2015. But her work was first introduced to me through two other women – Deborah and Erin. In the fall of 2013, a friend of mine forwarded me an email about a powerful grief ritual she had done at a spiritual community called the Findhorn Foundation in the north of Scotland with Sobonfu, and now two women were leading this same ritual in Colorado. I followed up immediately as this would be taking place in only five days. Again, just like knowing I had to draw the labyrinth on the beach, I also knew I had to do this grief ritual!

On my drive to the ritual, I saw a coyote on the side of the road and two strong elk. Seeing them was a welcomed blessing. I had slept the night before at my friend Selina's house as she lived closer to where the grief ritual was being held. I hardly slept because I was a jumble of nerves and excitement. In the morning, she wrapped me in her fake fur coat, something to help contain me and feel her support. Selina, a wonderful massage therapist, was also in Annie's training with me. She had gifted me numerous massage sessions since Michael's accident. She had my back in a few ways, and I now left with her coat around me.

I wouldn't need it later; we were blessed with a beautiful fall day where you peel off the layers you need in the mornings. The trees were in their full fall glory of brilliant bright yellows!

I had arrived and found myself in a small circle of thirteen people led by Deborah and Erin to begin this sacred work of grief. Deborah had studied with this amazing woman Sobonfu for many years and was leading these rituals herself. This grief ritual retreat took place near Lyons, Colorado, where Michael had his fateful fall. It felt right to be closer to the land where it all began. I was keenly aware of this when I signed up for the ritual. As soon as one says yes to attending a grief ritual, the process begins. They told us to pay keen attention to our dreams during this time. I could feel this process percolating in my bones; I was definitely ready to grieve.

What do I mean by 'I felt it in my bones'? After I said yes, it was as if I was closer to the trauma and my grief. And I felt nervous knowing I would be diving in with the group versus distracting myself from it. Thus, my grief felt closer than before. Sometimes I imagine it as a disheveled grubby human being who arrives at your door tattered and dirty (like *Shock*). It sets up camp on your front porch. And then it annoyingly knocks at your door or window until you open it. You see, all *Grief* wants is attention and acknowledgment. You have to be brave enough to invite this scary creature into your home and give it tea and cookies. Only then does it start to settle as you begin cultivating a relationship with it. Saying yes to this ritual settled my grief down – it just wanted to know I would give it attention by honoring it, sharing it, and letting it be witnessed by others who were also grieving.

Once I had said yes, I received instructions for the ritual. I was invited to write down on a piece of paper what I was grieving. We were told our grief items would not be returned to us. We couldn't include precious photos or anything else we wanted to keep because it would be burned at the end.

Instead of writing, I brought something else. Remember—I'm an artist and art therapist and I'm also a bit of a stubborn rebel and I needed something to show the enormity of the grief I was carrying inside me. I brought a square cardboard box that was about 15 inches wide. Inside, I placed other burnable items which represented my grief – this consisted of different colored tissue paper, other thicker paper, and a few other burnable bits and bots.

The largest item inside was a smaller box symbolizing our able-bodied sex life. At the time, this was what I seemed to be grieving the most. My vagina was physically aching at times. I felt its confusion and it too was grieving. Yes, the body grieves. (Note: it wasn't something that needed medical attention, but sometimes grief can do very strange things to the body, so it's a good idea to get a physical with a doctor or other wellness practitioner you know and trust if you are experiencing odd symptoms.)

The ritual happened over a weekend starting Saturday morning through midday Sunday. It was mid-October, and it was a beautiful weekend with warmer days and the oncoming cool nights. The retreat location was at Sunrise Ranch near the foothills of the Rocky Mountains.

On Saturday morning we introduced ourselves and spoke about what we were grieving. When it was my turn, I dramatically held the box upside down and let it all fall out in front of me. Out poured my mess of grief and I began to cry as my words attempted to leak out in between sobs and sighs. And I needed to do this – to bring something to show the enormity and mess of my grief. I needed to see a representation of what it felt like to be me on the inside and I needed this to be seen and witnessed. The group leaders were not pleased with the size of my box, but they worked with me to accommodate my needs. During the actual ceremony, I learned why—we were supposed to wrap our grief items entirely with black fabric. Luckily, they had a large enough piece to cover and contain my big grief box.

This was such a great example of how grief needs containment. Grief is messy, and I needed to have the mess mirrored back to me. Then I needed it to be contained in the box and then, later be contained in the ritual. Yes, grief needs containment, and, then and only then could I begin to set it down and release it.

The grief ritual retreat began with the group gathering in a circle to introduce ourselves and say what we were grieving. After this, Deborah and Erin spoke about grief and why we do this ritual according to the Dagara traditions. The Dagara is an indigenous tribe located in Burkina Faso in West Africa of which Sobonfu was a member and teacher. There is a lot I could say about the Dagara and grief. It could be a book in itself. To keep it brief, I will just say this: grief is a part of life and it's what makes us human. Thus, all we need to do is find a way to be with it—both alone and more importantly, in community.

They explained we would be creating specific altars or stations. There were three altars—one for ancestors, one for forgiveness, and lastly, the grief altar. The ancestor altar represented the strength and beauty of our lineages. It was decorated with fresh flowers, symbols of strength and love, photos of ancestors, and the color red. The forgiveness altar was decorated with flowers, symbols of water and flow, and the colors white, blue, and purple. The main altar was for grief itself. It was starkly decorated with white candles, a line of ash, and a backdrop of black fabric supported by tree branches. The ash was for protection, and it delineated the space between the grievers and the grief altar. Our items wrapped in black fabric would be tossed into this space.

Later I would learn in Elder Malidoma Somé's book, *Ritual: Power, Healing and Community*, this grief ritual, which was adapted for Westerners, was based on the traditional Dagara funeral ceremony.

There are many things I love about this ritual; one is that everything happened in the context of community. The altars were not put together by the leaders for us to just begin when we arrived. No, we as a community had to work together to create the ritual space. In fact, two years later, Sobonfu would put me in charge of creating the forgiveness altar at another ritual.

After the altars were ready, the leaders taught us the Dagara grief ritual song which we would sing over and over, until we no longer wanted to sing it. When I did this ritual later with Sobonfu, she said to us, "Eventually you'll hate this song and even hate me for making you sing it again and again because you'll be tired and weary and ready to be done."

The song had a specific purpose, actually, everything we did in ritual had intention. The song held the ritual together; it was a container itself. And if you weren't grieving at the altar or sitting in front of the other altars, you would be in the "village" singing and or drumming and even dancing. The song was sung in Dagara and the words were simple—"We can't do this alone."

When we were finally ready to begin, we lined up holding our grief items. The leaders began with an invocation to Spirit and the elements of the Dagara tradition: Fire, Water, Earth, Mineral, and Nature. Then we began to drum and sing the song in a procession to the grief altar where we'd place our grief items into the circle of ash. And once placed there, we could no longer reach in and get them back.

This was the beginning of letting go as we would then go through numerous rounds of grieving. We would grieve that afternoon, and then later after dinner, and then again before bedtime, and then we'd begin again in the morning. Years later, I would learn from Sobonfu that in her village in Africa, this would go on for days without any breaks – if you needed a break, you'd just take one.

After our grief items were all placed on the grief altar, we gathered in the "village" area, which was directly opposite the grief altar, and began to sing the song. Our job in the village was to keep the song going because it was what held the ritual together and supported the ones who were at the grief altar. The song felt like a gentle stream of water that kept flowing and it reminded us to keep our grief moving. The song itself comes from a story about a village that was flooded, and a man saw his wife and mother in the river both reaching for him to pull them out. He knew he could only save one. And this is where this song was born, out of immense grief and too much water.

When you felt the call to grieve, you'd go to the grief altar and express or emote it towards the altar. This looked like crying, raging, sighing, speaking, and even yelling, or just sitting there. According to the Dagara, grief is sustenance for the ancestors – it feeds them and in this way grieving is vital for our well-being and the well-being of our ancestors.

Our grief could look like many emotions or sensations with the obvious one being sadness. Sobonfu encouraged us to bring whatever emotion was coming through – anger, rage, confusion, sadness, and numbness. She even told us to go to the altar if we were feeling nothing. I remember one woman simply laying down in front of the grief altar and remaining there for hours just to be near her grief.

The first time doing this ritual at Sunrise Ranch with Deborah and Erin something quite extraordinary happened to me. One of the most beautiful parts of this ritual is when you go to the altar to grieve, someone from the village immediately follows you and stands directly behind you so you're never at the grief altar alone.

The first time I went to the grief altar and had someone directly behind me, I had a moment of remembering. It was as if I had already done this before in a previous life. And I also had an awareness that someday I'd be leading these very rituals.

The experience of knowing this was strengthened when I was asked to keep the drumbeat going. Deborah was drumming and I was standing beside her singing when she suddenly handed me the drum, looked me in the eyes, and said, "Keep the song going!"

I must've looked like a deer in the headlights as she rushed towards someone near the altar who seemed to be stuck in their process. I felt nervous to be suddenly given this role and there was a momentary glitch in the rhythm as I attempted to continue the drum beat while also singing the song. But I was pleasantly surprised at how easy it was for me to do this. I felt comfortable and empowered. *And this is when I knew in my bones, I'd be leading this ritual someday; I had found my soul's work and my life's calling. I would be centering my purpose on helping others grieve.*

After this ritual, I was hooked because what I learned was once we give grief this deep attention, a profound sense of gratitude and joy shows up. At the end of this ritual, I felt both exhausted and exhilarated, feeling both my grief and blissful gratitude. And this is when I began to cultivate a relationship to the word 'bittersweet,' and to the concept of both/and. My life was *both* bitter *and* sweet. And in this ritual, I could feel both. I was grateful Michael survived, and I was very sad about all the changes as a result. It was both/and, not either/or.

This ritual helped more than I thought it would. I haven't written about the details of this until now. Looking back, I have attended so many rituals I can't even count. Eventually, I went on to co-lead these with my friend Wendy Kaas a few years later. I became her 'wing-woman', and I just loved that. This ritual is sacred. I don't normally explain it in this much detail, and I never take photos of it. When I'm in a ritual space, it is sacred time, and it doesn't feel right to share it with others outside the space. But since this is an important part of my story, I will write more details here. I feel it's important to share this since the world is needing better grief practices, now more than ever. And I want Sobonfu's legacy of teaching Westerners how to grieve to carry on through me and the practice of grieving she gifted me.

Because I felt much lighter and could begin to feel joy again, participating in a grief ritual became a lifeline for me and I signed up for another one with Sobonfu herself. In February 2015, I traveled to Breitenbush Hotsprings in Oregon with Merryl to meet Sobonfu and experience the ritual with her.

Sobonfu became my friend, mentor, guide, and grief guru although she'd never call herself one. She taught me how to be with big emotions and it's because of her I now know how to hold space for others to grieve. Her grief ritual held me in my grief. And I continue to grieve for her because she passed away in January 2017. She's a blessed memory now. I had planned on attending more of her rituals – I had much more to learn from her.

Sobonfu was born and raised in Burkina Faso. She was an initiated member of the Dagara Tribe of West Africa. Her name means "keeper of ritual." Her skin was a deep chestnut brown, and she would wear clothes made from bright, bold, colorful African fabric with a matching headwrap. She was beautiful. She had the sweetest laugh and the most beautiful smile; when she smiled wide, you could see the distinctive gap in her front teeth.

Her voice was soft and melodic, and it soothed me when I needed it most and I could listen to her for hours. And when anyone sneezed, she would interrupt whoever was talking to say in Dagara, "Ashé." In her tradition, if anyone sneezed it was a sign the ancestors agreed or affirmed with whatever had just been said.

She had a small frame, and her bones seemed frail and tiny, yet she had a solidness to her presence perhaps due to leading grief rituals for most of her life. When I met her, due to some unknown condition, her organs were distended giving her a very enlarged belly. It was unnatural and I was concerned for her.

CHAPTER 17

GRIEVING LIKE A RACE HORSE

"Everything we love, we will lose."

—Francis Weller

The first time I met Sobonfu it was late at night, and she'd just arrived at Breitenbush Hot Springs and was in the backseat of a car. Merryl and I were walking to our quaint adorable yet rustic cabin when we saw her. Merryl reached inside the car to give her a quasi-hug and it was sweet to witness their love and affection. She had already been doing grief rituals with Sobonfu, and they knew each other well. When you meet someone in grief, you are friends for life; grief bonds are strong and deep.

I was nervous to meet Sobonfu, as I was also just nervous to do a grief ritual with about 60 people! But my nerves softened as I heard their fond greeting even though it was late, and she probably just wanted to go to bed.

I'm not sure why I was nervous to meet her. For some reason, I thought she might not be available for connection. This was not the case. She was open, sweet, and available. It was as if she knew me already – as if she was already my grief friend. She had the biggest heart along with the widest belly. Sometimes I wonder if she was holding onto all the grief from all the people she did grief rituals with over the years. She had led many and left a legacy of teaching many Westerners how to grieve. And for this, I will be forever grateful. Sobonfu – you taught me best how to grieve. You changed my life.

The next day at Breitenbush, we gathered in a large hall on the dark green well-worn carpet with this circle of about 60 other people. We were held by Sobonfu, the community she created, and by the thick log-cabin walls which surrounded and grounded me. We were also held and supported by the land and the waters. If you haven't been to Breitenbush,[7] it is beautiful in itself. It's nestled in the Northwest forests and has these amazing hot springs to get into after a long day of deep grief work. It was the perfect setting for grieving with a large group of people.

We gathered Friday night in a large circle. It was a much larger group than the one I attended in October 2013. I was intimidated by the size of the group, and I also wondered how we were going to grieve with this many people! We began with each person introducing themselves and their grief. Sobonfu invited the one who felt called to begin and then we would go in counterclockwise order. The person sitting two places away from me began, and I felt my stomach contract as I realized I would be the third to go out of sixty! I wanted to get up and run across the room so I would be last, but I didn't. When it was my turn, I simply said this: "My name is Beth, I'm from Boulder, Colorado and my partner crashed on his mountain bike, broke his neck, and is now a quadriplegic. Our life is upside down."

I kept it brief thinking about how many people had to speak. By the end of the circle, the intros were much more detailed, I wished I'd said I was grieving my able-bodied sexuality and had wanted to become pregnant.

---

[7] Breitenbush Hot Springs in Oregon was in a forest fire in 2020 and they lost forests and some of their original buildings. If you go now, it may look very different than when I was there in 2015.

One woman who appeared to be in her late sixties was sitting where I wish I'd been sitting, as she was almost at the end of the circle. Her name was Hillary Hurst and she'd been doing grief rituals with Sobonfu for many years. Her gaze was intense, her grey/black hair tightly woven into two thick long braids, and her voice was loud, gruff, and direct. And she got my attention when she started her intro with this, "If you're looking for grief support, this is fuckin' it!"

I immediately wanted to make friends with her because of her potty mouth and her passionate statement about this work. We did indeed become friends and we're still connected to this day.

The friends I have met in grief have the strongest bonds. Finding my grief peeps was one of the positive things which started to show up for me later. I call these positive takeaways the golden nuggets of grief. Yes, I'd lost some friends in my community, but now new ones were coming in. Hillary even gifted me one of her Tibetan mala necklaces. I wear it when I need to remember her support or when I am doing rituals and ceremonies. She was walking by me during a break and abruptly stopped, took off her necklace and placed it around my neck, and said, "This said it needed to be with you."

After hearing everyone's grief, there was a heaviness in the room, but this lifted when Sobonfu began to talk to us in her sweet voice about why it's important to grieve followed by an explanation of what we were about to do. She told us a story of how she came to know her life's purpose. She told us, "When I arrived in the United States, I was in New York City in a public bathroom stall. And I heard a woman sobbing in the stall next to mine. It was clear she was struggling because it was the kind of cry full of sobs and gasps. I waited for her to come out so I could ask her if she was all right. The woman simply smiled at me and said in a clear yet fake tone, 'I'm just fine, thanks.' That's when I knew I had to teach Westerners how to grieve."

Yes, we Westerners truly do suck at grief. We are experts at doing it privately in bathroom stalls or our cozy cars. But what we need to do is just allow ourselves to be fully human which includes letting ALL emotions be present including the negative ones. And we also need to learn how to come together to grieve in community. Everyone loses something – thus everyone grieves. Grief doesn't discriminate, it is what makes us human. In fact, everything we love, we will eventually lose someday.

Sobonfu taught me to grieve with my community; we do better when we do this together. And it can be done with sixty people! In fact, with all the other rituals I've done, I think it was this one that was the most impactful. First, it was the first time I grieved with Sobonfu herself. Secondly, sixty people were grieving everything from awful murders to losing a husband in an avalanche, to childhood abuse, baby loss, rape, loss of species and clean water, and even more. And we all had space to grieve, and it was as if the amount of grief in the room created momentum for more grief to show up. One of the reasons why grieving together is helpful is because hearing about someone else's grief can remind you of other grief you have.

Doing this grief ritual with Sobonfu, I felt like an eager racehorse who was beyond ready to bust out of the gate and run. I literally ran to the front of the grief altar after Sobonfu gave her beautiful invocation to the Dagara elements of fire, water, earth, mineral, and nature, and said the ritual was open. I had been ready for this and I needed a place to let out all my rage, and I did. I finally had a safe place where I could let the dragon fully express herself! I screamed and cried, and pounded my fists on the floor, I growled as snot dripped from my nose. I was messy. And it was such a relief to be in a room where grief was allowed to be feral and raw. Many people were grieving; there were three to four rows with about ten people per row.

It felt good to be there surrounded by many others who had the same amount of anger and rage as I had. I screamed so loud I lost my voice and felt pain in my chest. I pounded my fists hard on the floor and I gave myself bruises. (I learned to grab a pillow to pound instead of the hard floor even though it was covered in dark green carpet). I screamed and cried next to my friend Merryl who was grieving her pregnancy losses. We raged together and screamed at our ancestors demanding them to show up and support us. It was something I will never forget. And I would come to recognize when I needed to grieve in this way, I would feel a backlog of grief in me that would need to be tended to with this ritual. One of my favorite things Sobonfu would say was this, "You have to open the pipes of grief and let it flow, then there's more space for life and joy to come in."

I came back from the ritual at Breitenbush full of joy even though I still felt sad about my life situation. I found it hard to go back to work. Just like the rug had been pulled out from under me with Michael's accident, it also felt like the rug of my professional life was being ripped out and replaced. This ritual impacted me deeply. I questioned being in an office doing psychotherapy and found myself wanting to bring more nature and ritual into my work with clients. I started to dive deeper into Sobonfu's work and the Dagara cosmology and their indigenous technologies. It eventually led me to also work with her ex-husband, or as she humorously referred to him as her "was-band," Elder Malidoma Somé. It was the beginning of my shamanic healing path.

CHAPTER 18

OUR JOURNEY
TO THE ACCIDENT SITE

"Heaven and earth, the Celtic saying goes, are only three feet apart,
but in thin places that distance is even shorter. They are places that
make us feel something larger than ourselves, as though we are held in a
place between worlds, beyond experience."

—Kerri ní Dochartaigh

I n April 2015, I was beyond thrilled to learn Sobonfu would be coming
to Boulder to lead a grief ritual for the community. I was excited to
hear this because it meant Michael could attend, as he really needed it.
Some of our friends were excited to be a part of this, and even his sister,
Linda, flew out from Florida to join us. The day it was supposed to start,
we got a message it was canceled because Sobonfu's mother had died,
and she was on her way to Africa to grieve with her village.

I was disappointed to hear this yet happy to know Sobonfu was on
her way home to grieve. I was driving home from work when I got the
news. I pulled over to call Hillary (my 'this is fuckin' it friend). I called

her because I needed support around the new grief and help in holding a smaller ritual. I knew I needed to find a way to have this grief ritual even if it was just for a few of us. Plus, Michael's sister had flown from the east coast to be a part of this.

I started to wonder if I could host this ritual at my home as we were ready to grieve. I needed to do it with or without Sobonfu. Remember, once you say yes to doing a grief ritual, you start the process. I asked Hillary to sing the song in my voicemail to recall it later. Even though I'd sung the song a thousand times, I simply could not remember it on my own to sing for others. I think this was intentional since it is only used for ritual.

With the song in my head and my phone, we gathered to grieve in my living room: me, Michael, Tauna, Linda, and a few others. This is when I began to step into the role of holding this powerful ritual for my community. It was easy to do with a small group in my tiny home; we transformed our kitchen/living/dining room into a sacred ritual space. We cleared our kitchen island and transformed it into the ancestor altar full of photos and flowers. It was stunningly beautiful; beauty is a key ingredient in doing any ritual, yet even more important when doing a grief ritual.

Below the television on the east wall was our forgiveness altar and the grief altar was by our front windows facing south. We placed our grief items on the cherry wood chest made by one of my ancestors. We were cozy in grief together as the space was about 10 x 10 feet. We made it work, even though it wasn't as powerful as doing it with Sobonfu in person with a large group of grievers.

As I began to drum and sing the grief song in my living room, I was overcome with gratitude. Even though this was new for me, it felt right to be holding space for Michael and the others in this way. I felt honored to do this.

Sobonfu would return to Boulder in October of that year to lead a large group in yet another grief ritual. The timing was perfect for me. I would finish the ritual on Sunday and then board a plane Monday morning for Spain to walk part of the Camino de Santiago, a holy pilgrimage. It was as if Spirit had gotten a hold of my day planner and scribbled in these events back-to-back with a black Sharpie marker.

I asked Michael if he wanted to attend. He was hesitant to say yes to attending the entire weekend because of his nerves and the logistics of getting him there. His morning routine can take up to three hours or sometimes more depending on his needs and the pace of the caregiver. For this occasion, he wouldn't do his range of motion routine or as one caregiver named it, "cuddles and stretch." My morning routine includes cuddling with him in bed while he's getting stretched.

After cuddles and stretches, he gets put in his commode chair and is taken to the bathroom where his bowel routine is done and other morning care like brushing his teeth, washing his face, the things we all do. Then he's taken back to bed where his pants are put on and then he's put in his power wheelchair. Next is breakfast. We had to limit his routine to get to the grief ritual at a decent hour.

Michael decided to just go to the Friday night talk about grief. I was thrilled he finally got to meet Sobonfu. I introduced them and she said to me, "Is this your man?"

"Yes," I said with a proud smile on my face.

And, of course, they both fell in love with each other and began chatting away, touching on all kinds of things. Michael was moved by her talk about grief. He rolled over to me on rabbit speed, (rabbit speed is the fast setting on his chair) and said excitedly, "I want to figure out how I can come to the ritual tomorrow and Sunday."

Sobonfu had told us it was fine for him to arrive late because of his complicated morning routine.

The next day, Saturday, I arrived on time for the ritual and Sobonfu asked me, "Where's *my* man?"

I smiled and replied, "He's coming later, he's with his caregiver right now getting ready. I'll go get him in a bit."

Sobonfu smiled widely and said, "Oh good, I'm glad he's coming."

My dear friend Tauna came up to me and said, "Beth, I'll go get Michael, you stay here and grieve with Sobonfu."

I was a bit stunned by her offer as she had never driven Michael in our van, she was always hesitant to drive him anywhere. I replied, "Are you sure? You're okay getting him in the van and driving him here?"

She said, "Yes, it'll be a challenge, but I can do it because I don't feel much grief arising right now, and I want you to stay and not have to leave."

I gave her a huge embrace and said, "Thank you!"

I knew it would take a village to deal with Michael's situation and I was grateful our community was stepping up to help us out. Just like the grief ritual, we cannot do this quadriplegic life on our own.

While Tauna was off getting Michael, I was able to rage at the grief altar. Except this time, it was different. I felt like my grief was too much. My groans, moans, and yells were too intense for this group of grievers. I remember thinking, what the hell? Is Boulder too prim and proper to rage in this way? I was sitting next to an acquaintance of mine and as I began to scream and yell and cuss, she grabbed my hand and squeezed it with non-verbal approval. She later emailed me and thanked me for letting my rage out, and it made her question where her anger was. Yes, when you lose something dear to you, one healthy response is to be full of anger. It's the "protest emotions" as my grief mentor Alan Wolfelt calls them.

When Michael finally arrived, I noticed doing ritual with him present was different for me, I was overly attuned to him and his needs and now his grief. I noticed I didn't grieve as deeply as I had in the past. Or maybe since this was my 4th ritual, I wasn't as deep in grief as I had been when I felt like a racehorse bursting out of its gate.

It took Michael a while to feel his grief. When he finally felt ready to go to the grief altar I went with him, I supported him from behind. We actually took him out of the wheelchair for him to be at ground level at the altar with me supporting him to sit upright. And as soon as we were at the altar, suddenly there were a few people behind us. It felt amazing to not only support Michael at the grief altar but then for me to receive support as his caregiver and life partner. I realized then we also needed more support as a couple. It was beautiful to feel that the community had both of our backs.

Michael was mostly numb at the altar. He had a hard time feeling his grief because of the sheer amount of it. A few days prior he was also numb when we went to the actual site of the accident...

I had planned to get up to the accident site on the trail to gather some rocks to take with me on my upcoming Camino trip. I decided to leave a trail of accident-infused rocks with me as I walked in prayer. I wanted the rocks to linger on the Camino, to lay there with reverence and prayers; I needed the earth to help us grok it. The Camino could work its magic on the stones as I continued to heal in my way.

I had asked Michael if he wanted to come with me to gather rocks at the site of the accident. He could simply stay in the car as I collected them. The accident happened about a 1/2 mile or less up from the parking lot. It saddens me to think about this – he was almost down the trail he chose to ride that day.

Michael said yes to this inquiry. I was a bit stunned because he hadn't been open to this idea when I brought it up a few times before. I suggested we find a friend to be in the car with him while I went up the trail to gather my rocks.

I put a call out to our community to see if anyone would like to join me. I needed help with this piece as being at the accident site was still traumatic for both Michael and me as well. Many of our male friends said yes to this. None of my girlfriends could come and it will become clear as to why next.

When the time came to do this, we gathered at our house. Todd, Adam, Bruce, Steve, and David arrived to help us. We knew all of them from our contact improv community. We would do this difficult dance of getting him to where it all began. I started talking about the plan – about having them give Michael emotional support while I'd be gathering rocks and Todd simply blurted out, "Michael, do you want to go to the actual accident site?"

Michael was stunned and he took a long pensive pause as we all waited anxiously and leaned in for his answer. He surprisingly said, "Yes, I'm ready."

The next question was how.

Michael, ever the engineer, replied, "Could we use the sling that gets me in and out of my chair and bed to carry me up the hill somehow?"

I rushed to his bedroom to grab the yellow sling from his closet to show them. The sling has four loops or straps at each corner. There are two longer straps to hold his legs in place. Upon seeing the sling Todd asked, "Do you have two 2x4s?"

I responded, "I think we have one, let me text the neighbors to see if they have another one."

Turns out we had one in the garage, mixed in with all of the accessibility stuff plus everything else we hadn't dealt with since moving in together long ago – all the extra stuff that accumulates when you combine two separate households. I texted my neighbors who had a similar garage situation. And sure enough, they had one too. It really does take a village. And we were blessed to have community in our neighborhood.

Then I watched in awe of how the masculine gets things done as they started discussing just how we'd carry him up the mountain. Once Michael said yes to going up the trail, nothing could stop them, his "yes" set action into motion.

They planned to attach each loop of the sling to the 2x4s so they could carry him up the trail. He would hang in the middle of the 2x4s with each end of the boards propped on the shoulders of our male friends and be held into place with their arms and hands.

I led the way and the other male friend who wasn't carrying Michael was behind us all. We looked like a very different kind of procession as we somberly walked slowly and mindfully up the trail.

What a beautiful thing – to have this support for him and for us. To see him supported by the masculine as they carried him up the hill with him in the yellow sling, hanging down from the 2 x 4's, he looked like royalty.

When we arrived at the site of the accident, they put him down gently to allow him to fully take it in. They huddled around Michael, he had to lean on them to sit up. He was literally held by the masculine; he was supported both physically and emotionally as he was dealing with returning to where it all began.

He was numb and had a look of pure despair on his face. It was too much for him to take in and he appeared as if he wasn't fully present but was trying to be. He was not in his body and the look on his face changed to one of blankness and disassociation.

I started to wonder if it was too early to have brought him here. It was simply sad to see him; to feel him feeling into it and not wanting to feel it. It was discombobulating for him and just sad to witness and be there with him — where he was his last full able-bodied self.

This was really hard. Yet with Michael fully supported by five of his male friends, I was able to do what I needed to do. I performed ceremony as I lit sage and asked it to bless Michael and the land. I connected to Earth, the pine trees, and the large red slab of rock that started this journey. I then asked if I could take some rocks for my Camino trip and got a resounding yes even before I finished my question. (Sometimes the rocks say no to my request, and I always ask before I take them.) I collected about three handfuls of the red granite pebbles and stones.

While I was gathering rocks a few highly skilled mountain bikers came flying by us. Michael had more pain on his face and looked more checked out each time a biker whizzed by us. I'd never seen mountain bikers like that – and I now understood why Michael loved it. It looked as if they were flying as their wheels hardly seemed to touch the ground below them. They simply flew over the rock that caused the accident. I too felt slightly out of my body when I saw this.

With rocks gathered and Michael moving into the next phase of his healing journey, we began our slow descent down the trail. He had the courage to face his worst fears by going to the actual site, to the place where his body and soul fractured. It may have cleared the way for him to start grieving. Maybe it was this moment on the trail and meeting Sobonfu at her Friday night talk that led him to say yes to attending the grief ritual. He was finally ready to begin to feel his grief and process it; a process that would take many years. Eventually, the process would lead him to work with a shamanic practitioner for his healing.

I was pleased that Michael was able to begin his grief process by meeting Sobonfu and attending her grief ritual. As for me, my healing journey continued and the day after the ritual, with the Dagara grief song fresh in my brain, I would travel to Bilbao in the north of Spain where I would meet Rachael, Naomi, and the three other group members who would walk with me on the Camino. I would continue to come right side up. With my grief and joy freshly stirred up from the grief ritual, I'd take the first step of my 110-mile journey to walk in honor of my partner who no longer could.

CHAPTER 19

WALKING THE CAMINO

"Walk boldly through your life with an open, broken heart."

—Joanna Macy

Traveling to Spain went mostly well. Tears leaked out of the corners of my eyes every time I encountered Michael's able-bodied ghost along the way – arriving at the many airports, checking in, finding the gates, and getting on the planes. The last time I traveled with Michael was two years before the accident and we actually went to Spain. This felt especially hard – to be traveling internationally without him and to be returning to the place we had frolicked together.

My heart rate went up in Germany when I had to change planes in Frankfurt. The TSA officials searched my bag and were skeptical about my small bag of rocks. I couldn't understand what they were saying except for their body language and strange looks coming my way. They called their supervisor over who also gave me quite a stare, then he glanced down at the rocks, his body language softened, he smiled, muttered something in German, and then waved me through. I imagined he said this, "Oh another lovely rock person, she's fine." I'd like to be a

TSA agent just to see how many of us are rock people, it appeared he was one. I was hugely relieved as I'd been silently planning what to say about why I lugged them from the mountains of Colorado. Gratefully my rocks and I got on the next flight.

Two and half hours later the plane touched down amidst rainbows as we landed in the north of Spain, in the heart of Basque Country, which on a map looks like a shape of a heart! There seemed to be a hundred different shades of green covering the landscape; it looked like a patchwork quilt of farms below, and the sky was filled with thick rain clouds with the sun peeking through. Being greeted by a rainbow meant I was in the right place, and it seemed everything led me to this point— to the Camino for ten days of walking prayer.

I checked into my *la pension* in Bilbao around 2:00 p.m. where the bed was inviting me like a magnet to lay in it. I was exhausted from traveling but I resisted because I had to stay up to adjust to the new time zone. Everything in the room was pure white like a blank canvas as if white was the theme the interior decorator had in mind when creating the room. The sheets, duvet cover, pillows, curtains, furniture, walls, and even the artwork were pure white! The entire room shined brightly like light on a snowy spring overcast day. There was something beautiful about it; it was like crisp new paper to encourage your next creation. Like the brand new journal I had in my backpack waiting for me to fill it with insights from this journey.

I splashed water on my face, changed my clothes quickly, and went out to find a meal. My goals were simple – feed myself, go to the Guggenheim Museum to see the exhibit on Basquiat, stay up as long as possible, take a shower, and get to bed at a decent nighttime hour, although in Spain this is debatable as they stay up much later than we do. I went to bed feeling both excited and nervous. I would be meeting the group at noon tomorrow to drive to our destination to start walking the Camino.

If you've never heard of the Camino, I say welcome. The word Camino is Spanish for path, but it's much more than that. The Camino is a pilgrimage that has been walked by millions since the 8th century! It began as a path for animals and their shepherds and eventually became a pilgrimage for those on a spiritual or religious path. Saint Francis of Assisi walked it. By now, millions have walked this for many different reasons, it follows the milky way and was originally inspired by the stars.

When this path of stars fell into my orbit, I knew I had to make it possible. This was in August of 2015, and the trip was set for the end of October of the same year, only a few months later. I had to start raising money, it was going to cost me $1800 plus airfare. And more importantly, I had to get in shape; I started taking long walks every day because I'd be walking fifteen to possibly twenty-seven miles in one day!

I was surprised I'd never heard of the Camino before. How had I lived as long as I had without knowing about this amazing healing journey? I'd even lived in Europe once at the Findhorn Foundation, the very same community where Sobonfu had led grief rituals, and had never heard of it!

And just like the Dagara grief ritual, she calls to you when she knows you need her. I first learned of the Camino from my friend Naomi who mentioned she was co-leading this trip with her friend Rachael Corinne who led walking pilgrimage retreats. Naomi graciously offered to help me fundraise to make this trip possible. I felt a deep yes and took her up on her offer. And as soon as I posted my fundraiser, the money started pouring in from my community. Tears of gratitude fell from my eyes.

Once I had said yes to walking it, I suddenly felt something I hadn't in a while—joy, it felt like it was bursting out of my torso. With excitement in my belly, I started googling the Camino de Santiago. And funny enough, the first site I clicked on was from a man who discouraged you from walking it. It was an entire blog dedicated to dissing it for many reasons. I didn't let it stop me and I kept digging.

He didn't understand it was a spiritual pilgrimage, not just a backpacking trip or a trip to just work yourself physically, although it does indeed do this. The Camino challenged me on many different levels, and it was just what I needed to process my life and to come right side up again. It tested me physically, mentally, emotionally, and spiritually.

The Camino goes through these four challenges and many different regions. First, you are challenged physically as your body gets used to walking for 8-10 hours, or 15-25 miles a day. Then you are challenged mentally, then emotionally, and finally spiritually. Yet like grief, those stages could all happen simultaneously or out of sequence. And also, like grief, it all starts with being challenged physically; it starts with the body going into some kind of shock. And in my experience with grief, I was challenged in all ways all at once.

The first challenge for me on the Camino was the physical part; my feet hurt a lot. But walking was also enjoyable because of the beauty and the movement of walking all day. Then the mental and emotional challenges would consume me as I'd struggle with my thoughts and feelings. I wasn't used to just walking all day long. It was an all-day meditation; I watched my monkey mind go all over the place followed by my emotions tagging along after.

Walking the Camino is the perfect metaphor for the grief process itself and how these levels of the body and experience are challenged. And you have to let everything serve as medicine, even that which you'd like to be easier or different. Grief is also 'The Way,' and the trick is to see and use everything in your grief process as medicine, as a way to alchemize it into something of exquisite beauty and ultimately a process of growth and learning.

Naomi described her trip as a sacred walking prayer. And this is the best description for the Camino – it's a 500-mile-long prayer. The most popular route starts near the border between northern Spain and the south of France in a quaint medieval town called St Jean Pied du Port. It literally means 'the foot of the pass' and is located at the base of the Pyrenees Mountains. From there you walk five hundred miles to the west to the official destination—the cathedral in the city called Santiago de Compostela. Some people choose to walk an additional two days to the ocean to a town called Finisterre also known as the end of the Earth. It's right at the edge where land meets the ocean. It's literally the end of the trail.

Many other paths begin in other places, but they all end in Santiago. You could walk from Germany, England or Portugal if you wanted to. If you were to draw it, it would look like the lines on a scallop shell—with all the lines coming together at the narrow end of the shell. The ones who walk it wear the scallop shell to symbolize their pilgrimage. One who walks the Camino is called a "pilgrim" or "*peregrino*" in Spanish. The symbol of the scallop shell comes from the Catholic tradition – the coffin of St. James, the patron saint of the Camino, miraculously appeared washed up on the beach completely covered in scallop shells.

At the beginning of our journey, we were all given a shell and a pilgrim's passport to collect stamps from the places we stayed. If one walked the entire path, you presented your passport to the officials at the end to receive an official certificate. We attached the scallop shell to our backpacks to mark our pilgrim status, as if it wasn't obvious from our muddy boots, practical all-day walking outfits, backpacks, and walking sticks. The shell also had a practical use, you could use it to drink wine from vineyards along the way. One day, we came upon a wine fountain!

Some of the residents who lived near the Camino were super helpful, if they saw you were off the path or going the wrong way, they'd point you in the right direction. I only got lost once at a crossroads as it wasn't clearly marked by the signs along the way. In France, you followed the symbol of the shell or a horizontal red and white line to mark your way. In Spain, the symbol was a yellow arrow painted on the streets, sidewalks, trees, and buildings to make sure you never got lost. It helped and oh how I wished we had these symbols and other fellow human beings to show us the way when we get lost in the depths of grief.

My desire to walk was planted as a seed on my trip to Mexico when I was sent there in February of 2013. Remember when I walked all afternoon to the Mega Grocery store by accident? It was no accident as it made sense later when I found the Camino and my only purpose was to simply walk with my grief every day for 10 days. We only walked 110 miles or 177 kilometers. Most people choose to walk the entire thing which is about 485 miles or 780 kilometers and may take you about 30 days to do it, depending on your pace and if you take any rest days. We would end our time together in a town called Estella, named after the stars, where the ceiling of the cathedral was an intricate design of star shapes.

The terrain on the Camino was mixed from woodland trails to rocky paths, sidewalks, and the edge of highways at times. Most of the paths were on country roads or well-worn trails in wooded areas. The scenery was stunning most of the time and it was beautiful to take in the landscape along the way. It was a pleasure to notice the changes slowly, unlike when you're in a car and the landscape is a blur out the window. The Camino asks you to take your time; notice the beauty all around you and then go inward and contemplate the reason why you were called to walk it. I met many others who were also walking to figure out their lives after a sudden loss.

We stayed in *los albergues* (hostels in Spanish) which were specifically geared towards pilgrims. They catered to us by providing either an extravagant or simple dinner that always came with really good wine which is part of the culture in France and Spain. These hostels also did our laundry and even folded it for us. The beds were simple; there would either be a few in one room or sometimes you'd be sleeping in bunk beds with about 20 other people. Earplugs were a necessity because inevitably someone would be snoring. We did stay a few nights in posh hotels, which was such a treat; luxuriating in the solo-ness of not having to share space with others.

The day we met up as a group in Bilbao we did brief intros after we piled into the van driven by a small Basque man with rosy cheeks and a smile so wide it radiated into his eyes. He was very proud of his Basque heritage and language; he taught us a few phrases. He was also fluent in both Spanish and French. We drove a few hours through the green landscape, the one that looked like a quilt from above. Again, it was both rainy and clear with patches of sunlight and then dense clouds with a few scattered rainbows. We drove into France and started our journey there.

We were dropped off at an old Catholic church surrounded by a cemetery which was being cleaned and prepped for All Saints Day where the dead are honored with fresh flowers. We were able to fill up our water bottles if we needed to. The Camino has many drinkable water stations along the way, which was great – we didn't have to carry an entire day's worth of water.

The woman who held us all was Rachael Corinne Sanborn who was super smart, witty, and Camino savvy. She was like a Camino Fairy, when she walked it looked as if she was floating – she was a trained dancer in traditional Balinese dance and she walked with tennis shoes with hardly any support, yet she never felt any pain. She had already walked this path numerous times and she spoke Spanish fluently and beautifully. I felt safe to be in her care.

We circled up quickly with our backpacks on and stated our intentions for walking that afternoon. Rachael had us gather every morning and state our intentions. Today's first day of walking was just a warmup – we only walked eight miles compared to eighteen or twenty. As we started to walk the sun came out fully. The lolling countryside greeted us as we walked up and down tiny hills like a slow-motion roller coaster. We walked amidst large trees, forests, and corn fields that were way beyond harvesting time.

I had put all my rocks into the pocket attached to my backpack's waistband, this way they were accessible when I felt inspired to drop one on the trail. I also stuck Michael's gumby toy at the top of one of the shoulder straps, he was right next to my head and heart. Michael made a point of giving me something of his to take with me. I also placed in another pocket a small angel troll given to me by a dear art therapy mentor and friend, Sue Wallingford.

The first place I dropped one of my rocks was at a stream we crossed after we passed an old cottage that had an empty power wheelchair in their front yard. I immediately thought of Michael and my grief suddenly gathered in my throat. I cried as I tossed the rock into the water from the bridge and whispered to the moving waters below me, "Help us lighten this heavy load we've been asked to carry."

I placed more rocks on some of the markers made from concrete along the way. I was inspired by others who built rock cairns or other piles of small stones – I wasn't the only rock person walking the Camino. I would leave one small pebble when I saw other gatherings of stones like this. I even placed one at the foot of a Mother Mary statue, her feet wrapped with a snake, inside one of the cathedrals along the way. Others had done the same. I intended to leave behind a trail of the accident stones on this prayer path to help us digest the immense losses we were going through.

Our destination for the afternoon was a small medieval town called Navarrenx where we stayed at a very special hostel called L'Alchimiste, The Alchemist. The owner was a handsome Frenchman, Jeán Geatán, an artist whose work was everywhere. The entire place was a piece of art. He bought this old cottage to get away from the busyness of city life and devoted his life to making art and studying the process of alchemy.

Alchemy is the scientific art rooted in medieval times of turning one matter into another such as transforming lead into gold. It is the perfect metaphor for walking with grief, hoping sorrow would transform into joy.

Eventually, Jeán opened his home to the pilgrims coming by as it was right on the Camino path. He only accepts donations to stay there. Outside the front door, he created a tree-like sculpture with hiking boots, an invitation to take off your shoes and rest a while.

His place was sweet and inviting, inside it was lit up with soft light from lamps he created from tree roots, stumps, and resin. My bedroom had a lamp made from an upside-down basket, dispersing the light in a pattern all across the room, like stars on a clear night. Each nook and cranny was arranged artistically and he hung inspiring French phrases related to alchemy such as, "L' impossible reste à faire." Which means – the impossible remains to be done. We would see these, and other phrases later hung along the Camino on trees as reminders to keep walking and keep going inward to contemplate the changes of life.

Our dinner was an artistic delicious five-course meal gathered around a low table near the large hearth where an inviting warm fire was roaring. The napkins were neatly folded into small origami hearts and the carrots in the salad were carved into the word CAMINO. He then spoke to us in French about the alchemical process of being on the Path. It seemed everything this man said or touched became art. I felt held by him, his beautiful French, (even though I didn't understand most of it,) his food, the warm fire, and the ambiance of his home.

Breakfast the next morning was at 7:00 a.m. We gathered around a long wooden table for a simple pilgrim's breakfast which most often consisted only of homemade bread, butter, jam, yogurt, and coffee with milk served in small bowls, a French custom. If we were lucky there'd be cold cuts, cheese, and hard-boiled eggs. I would pack some in my backpack later for a snack. Somehow, I learned to subsist on bread and butter as I was used to eating way more protein for breakfast; I was missing my bacon and eggs.

I am not a morning person. It was a challenge for me to get up this early, be on time, and be packed and ready for the day. I packed what I needed in my backpack and the rest was hurriedly stuffed into another small suitcase. Thankfully we hired a baggage porter service to drive our extra baggage to our next destination. It was a relief to know I wouldn't have to carry everything in my backpack.

When I was reading about the Camino there was debate about what it meant to be a true pilgrim. Some believed you needed to carry everything you had with you. And others believed you could hire the bag porter service. When I learned our trip would include this service, I didn't debate it at all. I was already carrying a heavy load of grief. I instantly said yes to the baggage carrier service. I was learning it was okay to ask for help and why make it harder than it had to be?

My main stress with this was having the right timing for my morning poop. I didn't want to poop on the trail, which you could do if you absolutely had to. My body adapted to this eventually. It's amazing what the body can do when it needs to.

Promptly after breakfast and morning hygiene routines we gathered in our morning circle on the trail to state our intentions for the day. Rachael read a poem or other inspirational quote with a certain theme. My intention for this day was to be present and to walk with beauty and gratitude. I also thanked Spirit for making it possible for me to be here, to be in an able body, and to have the ability to walk. Because Michael no longer had the use of his able body, I was keenly aware of all my able body did for me.

We started walking around 8:00 a.m., which was the goal every morning. Sometimes we started even earlier depending on how many miles we'd be walking on that day. If we were blessed with a clear day, we walked with our morning shadows as the sun was rising behind us. We walked towards the west and followed the path of the sun and toward the evening if we were lucky, we'd see amazing sunsets.

Lunch was taken along the Camino. This day we stopped next to farm fields and brought out our lunch which had been divided into any extra space in our backpacks. We set out a smorgasbord of bread, butter, cheeses, cold cuts, a few veggies, apples, pears, cookies, and chocolate. On our way out of town in the morning we'd buy fresh baguettes and stuff them into someone's backpack. One day we even came upon a baguette vending machine!

While cutting the cheese and apples, I cut my middle finger badly and it took a while for the blood to stop. We bandaged it up with our first-aid kits. Later while walking it began to throb with pain especially because my hand was in the down position while walking most of the time. I started holding it up and it felt like I was telling the world to fuck off. And actually, I was because I was very angry about losing so much in my life. I thought about this as I walked and wondered if I could transform my anger into something softer. Could I really alchemize my rage into love? Was that possible?

I walked by a farmer in a combine harvester machine; he was working the large corn fields and it reminded me of my mother's lineage – my grandparents Kate and Vic who were farmers in Nebraska who came from farmers in Odessa, Ukraine, and Kutter, Russia, who all came from farmers in Germany back in the 1700's. I thought of my mom and the amount of grief she had of losing both of her parents within one week. I then felt my grief – I lost both my maternal grandparents when I was only ten years old; I wished I had known them longer. I walked with this grief and then I simply began to drop into a place of gratitude for them and all my ancestors for giving me this sweet life, even the hardship of this one precious life that we'd been given.

Later that night in a pre-sleep, hypnagogic state, I realized I'd already been on this path since the accident – somehow, I had been choosing beauty and gratitude amongst the suffering. I drifted into a deep sleep with full long dreams. There was no need for sleep meds here, walking all day was a cure for that.

The next day was a long one. It was our first full day of walking; we walked 19 miles! During lunch, Rachael proposed we walk off the path a bit and up a hill to a special shrine overlooking the valley with the Pyrenees in the distance. This beautiful side trip meant we'd be walking into dusk and possibly finding our next *albergue* in the dark. We all agreed this uphill detour was worth it. Normally we walked until 4:30 or 5:00 p.m. depending on how fast you walked and how many breaks we'd take.

We started our trek up the hill, and I thought we were such dedicated pilgrims – to add more miles up a hill nonetheless for this extra trip. We encountered large honey-colored cows and big horned bulls and had to be escorted through them by the rancher. This got my adrenaline going, I had never been that close to cows like that before.

At the top after taking in the view and visiting the shrine, we sat on the green grass abundant with blooming purple crocus flowers and shared why we said yes to walking this prayer pilgrimage. The group I walked with was small—a Swiss woman who I adored, a woman from California who annoyed me, and a man from the East Coast who reminded me of a challenging relationship with a male friend.

The Swiss woman was walking because of a big transition in her career and her relationship. The man had signed up at the last minute and was simply walking to enjoy the food and wine! Like, did he not read it was a 'walking prayer pilgrimage'? I was very annoyed by this. I believe it upset me because I was jealous – I wished my goal could have been as simple as his. But no, I'm here to walk with my heavy amount of grief.

I don't remember what the California woman's purpose was. She annoyed me the most. For one, she was a strict vegan. Now, I don't have anything against people who are vegan, how and what you eat is your decision. However, on the Camino one has to put a lot of effort into that food lifestyle because, for the most part, the food along the Camino was animal-based. This meant Rachael had to go out of her way to buy special food for her and sometimes she didn't even want the bean patties! It was nearly impossible to be a pure vegan on the Camino. I traveled to Europe for the first time right after college and at that time I had been vegetarian for about a year and was subsisting mainly on bagels and way too much cheese. My mom had asked me anxiously, "You're not gonna be a vegetarian on your trip, are you?"

I said no, and she was relieved. She is such a foodie and loves to cook because she loves to eat. She replied, sighing out like she'd been holding her breath for my answer, "Oh good, eating is a huge part of traveling to Europe, and the meat and cheese is really good over there. I didn't want you to miss out on any of it."

Inevitably every evening on the Camino this vegan woman from California had to have her questions translated to the hosts. What's in the soup? Is it made with butter? Is it made with meat broth? Sometimes this meant the hosts would have to go make a special dish just for her.

But what annoyed me the most was on the second evening as I was talking about losing Michael to quadriplegia, she interrupted me to share she was moved by a similar story she'd recently seen on Oprah's Soulful Sunday program. She went on and on about this and the conversation never came back to me. That night we were also a larger group as other pilgrims were staying at the hostel. Eventually, everyone left the dinner table, and I was left sitting there with Rachael who turned to me sweetly and said, "Beth, I'm sorry you got interrupted, do you want to share the rest of your story? I'd love to hear it."

I continued with tears in my eyes and was appreciative of her picking up where I had left off. I learned then it seemed it was just easier for some people to relate to these stories through the comfortable gap between them and technology versus hearing it from a live warm human being in real life. My story was too much for this woman who challenged me. And I thought – I should be on Oprah's show!

I was annoyed by her because I was easily upset by many little things at this time. She had told me more than once I should dye my hair. I started going gray in my 30s and at this time I was even grayer; I blamed it on the stress, trauma, and grief of everything.

This woman was tuned into her Facebook friends more than our little group. I think her purpose for walking the Camino was only to share it live with her entire network. I never once signed onto social media and was ecstatic to have a reason not to. I tuned in deeper into my process and into a different kind of network– Nature, the beauty around me, and the people who walked it with me. I was simply learning who I could trust on this trip – the leaders Rachael and Naomi and the woman from Switzerland. The other two just annoyed me and I didn't trust them with my story.

Were they truly obnoxious or was my perception of others clouded by my own grief process? Probably the latter. And actually, I made peace with the man who just wanted to drink good wine, his presence eventually reminded me that sometimes we just need to do something just for the sheer pleasure and joy of it. He was medicine for me too because he reminded me of a male friend who I'd tried to reconcile our relationship with to no avail and I was left to process it on my own. And thinking about this on the Camino was the perfect time to do this as I had hours to process everything entering my brain.

After our circle of introductions on the hill filled with purple crocus flowers, we walked down and continued to our next *albergue*. We walked with the setting sun, through dusk and into the dark. It was quite majestical to watch the light fade and attune to using our senses differently. My eyes adjusted to the lack of light as the world became more two-dimensional. We came upon a sight that confused me. It seemed to be moving and the closer I got to it, I realized it was a tall white horse. It was like an angelic Camino guardian lighting our path. I could see its breath in the cool air when it neighed, and it may have been frightened by us as well.

I was grateful to be walking in the dark and we were lucky for a clear night sky. We were led by the Milky Way with the stars shining above us. It was truly magical.

What I shared at this moment on the hill with those crocuses and my small group as witnesses was this – I was walking with a very specific purpose – to be with my grief and to walk because my partner no longer could. Walking the Camino was one of the hardest things I've ever done to process the worst thing that ever happened to me. Michael and I had lost so much – our able-bodied relationship and the dream of having a child together. And then we had to grok how to deal with this confusing new life because it wasn't a death loss, yet so much had died.

I came to realize grieving is a privilege. It's a gift to ourselves if we have both time and resources to take space out of real life to process it. I was acutely aware of the gift I'd given myself to walk the Camino and I pondered this as we got closer to the mountain.

CHAPTER 20

WALKING
UP THE MOUNTAIN

"You're off to great places. Today is your day.
Your mountain is waiting so get on your way."

—Dr. Seuss

Yes, indeed the mountain was waiting for us. We'd been walking towards this mountain range for three days and now we were nestled at the bottom of it in the town of Saint-Jean-Pied-de-Port. Walking into this town through the thick medieval gate was like walking back in time. We found ourselves on a narrow ancient pedestrian path made of square cobblestones interspersed with shining metal blocks engraved with the Camino scallop shell. Suddenly the path was full of people, both tourists and excited new pilgrims who were prepping for their first day of walking all day uphill. There was a palpable buzz of excitement.

I appreciated Rachael even more as the three days of walking up and down the gentle hillsides in France had prepared us to walk all day up a mountain. I was also feeling ready to wrestle with my emotions and thoughts that were starting to speak up because by now my body was used to the physical pain of walking all day.

I found my group at the official Camino office where one entire wall was filled with a map of the trek we were about to tackle the next day. The size of the map was appropriate – this was a huge and daunting task. We also had to officially check in because they needed to know who was walking the mountain path and who would be walking the valley trail. There are two options because sometimes the weather is so bad, they have to close down the mountain path. It can be extremely dangerous; pilgrims have gotten lost and even died along the mountain trail.

The weather forecast was written in multiple languages so each of us could decide which route to take. One could also ask as many questions as needed, with the many dedicated volunteers bustling around the place.

We arrived earlier in the afternoon that day to just be tourists. We had extra time to go see the Gothic Cathedral near a medieval bridge and do some shopping if we wanted to. We met up later in a bar and then we took a taxi to our next hostel which was a few miles up from the town center. I was happy to shave off an uphill mile or two to have an easier start the next morning.

We got off earlier than usual the next day and by now I was used to this frenzied morning routine. It was a beautiful day. It was sunny and clear yet slightly windy. I felt nervous but ready for the journey up. I thought of my paternal grandparents' favorite bible verse – "This is the day the Lord has made, let us rejoice and be glad in it." Psalm 118:24.

This was indeed the day, and I was trying to be glad–in–it because right away we walked up a very steep incline. I started walking with the Dagara grief song which was still fresh in my mind and heart but that wasn't the only thing I walked with. I also walked with the three-word mantra I'd been using for many years before this, three small words but really hard to practice—"Love What Is." But just how do I love quadriplegia?

With my mantra as a huge fat jawbreaker in my mouth, I grappled with it as I walked. I sucked on it all day as I tried to take it in and grok it. How do I love quadriplegia? How do I love this life? I love Michael, but I don't love disability. Who does? I wanted to spit it out, I hated the way it made my life taste—sour and bitter.

And with jawbreakers – if you try to chew it into smaller bits, it actually hurts to crack it open with your jaw, so you have to patiently suck it. You can't force it. Just like big grief – you have to digest it slowly to be able to integrate it.

And to be honest, I was scared to walk all day up a mountain. Yet that is what living with quadriplegia felt like. Heck, this is what grief feels like. My life felt like I'd been dropped into the middle of the wilderness with no map. I had a few provisions – water, some food, extra layers, a flashlight, and the jawbreaker to suck on. The hard, big sour piece of candy I wanted to spit out but couldn't, I didn't have a choice. I had to keep sucking it.

The thing about the Camino is if you're walking to understand your life and your grief the Camino will challenge you. If you're open to this, then you're likely going to have many insights and synchronicities along the way. If you aren't ready to receive every single interaction and challenge on the Camino as medicine, then, frankly it will spit you out. You must be willing to receive its magic. It's like walking along an acupuncture meridian of the earth, but it is you who receives both the pain and blessing of the needle.

I walked up the mountain all day chewing on the words—love what is. The mountain reached up to me at every step. The trail, the way, had my feet. It met me. The beauty was stunning, along the way, I saw far below the green lush fields – both wild and farmed. I felt in awe of the scenery. We had a bird's eye view because of how high we were; it took my breath away, or perhaps it was the incline.

The higher up we got, the more the wind blew. I walked with a stick I had found a few days prior. I bonded with it as it became my walking companion. I decorated it with my inspiring ribbons which had been knotted together. I brought them to leave along the trail, they were prayers and markers for specific people who wanted special Camino blessings. They were like cloth cairns guiding me and others along my way and I would leave them in certain places where others had done the same. I wasn't the only one leaving a trail of prayers behind.

We took a slight side trip to visit a shrine to Mother Mary on some rocks. I reached into my bag in the front of my pack and placed a rock with baby Jesus on her chest. Again, there were many mementos left from others as well. I said my prayer into the wind, "Please Mama, hold us as we continue to walk and roll through this path given to us. And thank you for this opportunity to be here on this mountain."

At this point walking the Camino put me in a kind of trance-like state. And I remember the pain was intense when I'd put my foot onto the ground and be one step closer to my destination, I'd focus on my foot being in the air. And I said out loud to myself, "In the air…no pain… my feet have wings."

I would say "flying feet" or "no pain." And I would focus on the lack of pain when my feet were a few inches in the air above the trail. I had to do this for quite a while because each step was excruciating. I could fully feel my feet through the pain I felt, and it immediately connected me back to Michael who could no longer feel his feet at all.

And even though I was in a lot of pain, my walking was a prayer and an offering. It was a way of connecting to the land, to Mama Gaia, to Spirit, and the mystery. Walking along this path of stars, it was guided by the light as I was too. With each step, I began to trust my life again, even this life. And each step was giving me the wisdom to deal with hardship – just put one foot in front of the other and just – keep – going. We passed a sign that said this, and I saw it right when I needed it.

The Camino also reunited me with my pen and paper. I hadn't been able to write in my journal at the time of the accident. At some point, I started a journal on my computer where the words flowed out of me through the clickity taps of the keyboard. But on this journey, I left the digital behind to allow me to tune in deeper to a path that had been walked for centuries and tread upon by millions of footsteps. And each footstep I took was infused with the ones who'd walked this path before me. I was joining the river, the current of the ones who also had walked with their hearts in pieces and sought to be put back together in some kind of order or assemblage of a doable life. But to be honest, I was often too exhausted to write long entries in my journal like I used to before the accident. I jotted down the highlights and lowlights of the things I wanted to remember in short bullets. This day would have the most bullets.

Once we started walking, we would naturally fall into a group rhythm where we'd have time to walk with a partner and time alone. I preferred to walk mostly alone yet I was never truly by myself. I was also walking with my *Grief*, yes, she was there every step of the way, also complaining and struggling. Yet somehow walking all day settled her. She felt at home with Nature all around. She wore well-worn hiking shoes and had two fancy walking sticks, and a wide-brimmed sun hat cinched to her head. And even though her feet hurt, she was beginning to feel less emotional pain as well.

I collected feathers along the way. In fact, feathers seemed to be a theme on this trip. I had oddly found one under my seat on my flight to Europe. Then I saw another one painted large on a billboard outside Bilbao. And then later I started seeing them all along the trail.

I began to gather some of these feathers and on this day, I attached a medium-sized white one to the top of my walking stick. I simply stuck it into the crack, I thought for sure it would fly off because of the strong winds which seemed to be getting stronger the higher we climbed. I began to watch it – it was like a game; a most welcomed distraction to keep me going.

The wind was fierce – the kind that blows through you and puts a chill into your bones. Yet somehow the wind was comforting even with its relentless obnoxious presence. It was like grief itself – hitting you down to your bones, chilling your soul, and never stopping, always present, and even more present while walking in the tundra-scape. The higher we got, the fewer trees we saw. These trees all were slanted in the same direction with growth only on one side from years of blowing winds. The trees seemed to be replaced by wild horses wearing bells. They were a beautiful sight to behold and to walk with for a short while. And the sound of their bells was mesmerizing. We stopped to have lunch near some of these horses. It was the fastest lunch ever as the wind didn't take a lunch break. We huddled beneath some boulders we found to make the most of it.

The wind was so strong you could lean into it. It reminded me sometimes all you can do in grief is just lean into it. In this way, it was an odd, welcome friend and served as a reminder for becoming friends with grief. I couldn't make the wind stop, and I couldn't find a way out of its presence, I simply had to find a way to make peace with it. I had to love the wind. It became the day I began to make friends with quadriplegia, which also was like an annoying relentless wind.

There was a warming hut near the top of the mountain where you could take a small reprieve from the relentlessness of the weather. Another reminder to take breaks from grief too. Yet this hut wasn't luxurious at all, also like grief. You can pause but it ain't pretty. The hut had four walls and small openings for windows. It had remnants of others making fires to warm up and they also left lots of trash behind. We entered and paused for about ten minutes to get a break from the wind blasting at our uncovered skin.

Back on the path I was simply in awe of the white feather at the top of my stick – it just simply held on! It never blew off. And I realized it was a symbol for me. I didn't give up either. I held on even when the path got harder and steeper. I was present and I stayed with Michael no matter what. It was surprisingly strong as it wasn't really attached in any way. I started watching it more closely after I realized it was a symbol of myself. The feather was walking with me, my stick, and the wind up this mountain path. And it never blew away as I kept expecting it would. I kept watching and waiting. Huge gusts of wind would blow, and I would be so concerned about my safety and comfort I'd forget to look at it. And then I'd look, and she would still be there hanging on, just like me.

At some point I decided if she didn't blow off at the top of the pass, I would free her and let her live on the top of the beautiful mountain landscape. I let her go at one point along the path in a forest full of birch and beech trees. I thanked her for walking with me the entire way up and holding on, and then I let her go. I wasn't attached to this feather. And I wanted it to remain here amongst this beauty to remember this place even more. It's like the scene in the movie *Harold and Maude* when Harold gives Maude a note which says, "Harold loves Maude." She holds it close to her heart and says, "And Maude loves Harold. This is the nicest present I've received in years."

And then she immediately throws it into the water. Harold is shocked and she looks at him lovingly and says, "So I'll always know where it is."

Like Maude I said a prayer too as I let the feather fly away in the wind, I whispered, "Thank you for reminding me that I too can hold on no matter how hard this path gets. Thank you, thank you beautiful feather. Go find your place amongst the trees now."

Sometime after this, I saw a small sign that told me I was now in Spain. It was so small I almost missed it. And then a little while later I was at the top of the mountain at an elevation of 1450 meters or 4757 feet. To me, this seemed like nothing as I lived near Denver which is known as the mile-high city at 5280 feet above sea level. The journey was epic, it felt like I'd climbed a fourteener. The trail then had a steep decline, the guidebook even says this – be careful, injury is common on the steep downhill part into Roncesvalles when your mind and muscles will be tired – stay extremely focused.

At this point, I was very attentive to my thoughts and feelings as I came to what was like clockwork every day on the Camino where I'd hit a wall. On our descent, amidst the thick beech tree forest, the trail was piled high with fallen leaves. The leaves had collected over time and the path and forest floor were covered in about two feet of orange and brown leaves.

It was as if some divine presence laid out a cushion of leaves for us. Did it know I was about to hit that wall? Nearly every afternoon on the Camino, regardless of what kind of terrain we were on, I would hit my emotional, physical, and mental walls and be ready to be done. I wanted to protest and sit down and not walk anymore. I wanted to stop like I did when I was a six-year-old learning how to ski. But I had to persevere at this point because no one in my small group was behind me, and I couldn't just take off my skis and slide down on my ass as I did when I was six.

Regardless, it was such a delight to walk in the thick leaves which felt like a red carpet laid out before us that seemed to say, "Thanks, we honor your trek up the mountain, now all you have to do is walk down."

The magical distraction of the leaves helped me, and I smiled and felt like a child again as I kicked the leaves around and enjoyed the sound of my feet rustling through what appeared like two feet of snow. It helped me to continue to just walk down to my next destination which was the famous monastery and hotel in Roncesvalles, Spain.

Another most welcomed distraction was a small group of miniature wild horses who were scattered amongst the forest and rocks. They also wore bells around their necks that would chime as they moved and chewed their food. It was such a sweet sound to serenade my descent.

My goal for the day was more than just arriving at my destination. Today I wanted to get to the monastery where they held a special mass every day for pilgrims. The idea of attending this followed by a warm meal with a glass of red wine was my carrot dangling in front of me to keep me going. That and the pleasure of not walking. And hopefully, a room with a bathtub so I could soak my cold and tired bones, especially my aching feet.

As I made my way down, each step was filled with more agony even though with each step I knew I was closer to the hotel. My feet hurt so much that at this point all I could do was feel the pain. The pain felt as if it was lingering up and into my legs, to my knees, and into my hips. Then, suddenly I was full of anger. The group leader had gone ahead of me, which I had been okay with, we had checked in about this. And the other leader had to take the bus because of excruciating pain showing up in her Achilles. I knew I was the last one of our group on the trail and at this point, I simply felt angry I was all alone.

I started ranting and raving, and I hit my walking stick hard on the ground. I hit it so hard it broke into two pieces, one part flew over the edge and then tumbled down the mountainside. My rage then turned into sadness; I had become attached to my walking companion called a stick. I began to feel more of my rage and anger about the pain in my feet, then the fact that I still had to walk, then the fact that I was alone and felt left behind. I was transported to having to burn through old emotions linked to this – being born with hip dysplasia, I was often left behind. I grew up with two brothers and was often left out. I was given the opportunity to process this on the trail where I could see the sun beginning to set. Fear started to walk with me too and my mind began to spin out with all kinds of questions – what if I don't make it? What if I'm lost? What if I never find my group again?

My thoughts eventually looped back to my life with Michael and our situation. And I would feel my grief, loss and sadness, and anger about his accident and how we now had to find a way to live with quadriplegia. I didn't ever question my love for him nor my decision to stay with him either. I never doubted us, I only questioned how we were going to do this, and I wondered what it was going to be like and just how hard it would be. And more importantly, did I have the strength and stamina to do it?

CHAPTER 21

MY PILGRIM'S BLESSING

*"The heart that breaks open can contain the
entire universe."*

—Joanna Macy

E xhausted on all levels as I came around the corner, the beech trees
began to thin out to reveal a most welcome site – civilization! As I
crossed a tiny babbling brook I could see the famous Roncesvalles Hotel,
Cathedral, and Monastery. This meant – warmth, respite, food, and a
well-deserved glass of wine. I was the last one to stumble into the hotel
that had long awaited me on the day's journey up and over the Pyrenees
and up and over into Spain.

It was late in the afternoon, 4:30 or 5:00 p.m. when I finally came
in the double doors of the famous hotel and peeked into the bar to find
my group. They were all huddled around a small wooden table near a
roaring fire in this quaint centuries-old tavern. It was a small room with
high ceilings and thick dark wood beams. The walls were made of stones
almost two feet thick. The floor was made of earthy orange tiles and the
walls were covered in wood paneling. It was a perfect place to hold me

after one of the most challenging days on the Camino. However, it was packed full of people with loud chatter encouraged by flowing beers, spirits, and wine. The environment was too stark of contrast for having just come from the path where the only sounds I heard were the crunching trail beneath me, a slight breeze in the trees, and a few birds singing.

I hardly said much to my group. I just wanted them to know I had arrived safely and then I quickly left. I was determined to get my pilgrim's blessing. I found my extra bag, jealous of its easy journey, and lugged it up the wide wooden and well-worn warped stairwell from thousands of years of weary travelers. I was always really happy to see my extra bag at the end of the day. It had all my other necessities and most importantly it carried my other shoes that my feet were extra happy to slip into after being stuck in hiking boots all day. It was also very pleasing to put on dry clean socks as well as evening attire which consisted of soft black leggings and a comfy light green tunic. The Camino was reuniting me with simple pleasures – who knew clean, dry socks could be so pleasurable?

I quickly surveyed my cozy room. It had a long European bathtub and a separate bidet! I love bidets, they are assholes' best friend as it makes much more sense to clean yourself with water instead of harsh toilet paper. I knew I'd have a long bath later and was looking forward to it as well as a pleasant shit the next morning.

After viewing the bathroom and taking off my hiking shoes and sweaty socks, I proceeded to do what I always did upon arrival, I laid on the floor and placed my feet up the wall, and took a moment just to rest. But then I realized I needed to find the mass. I'm not Catholic, nor very religious in a traditional sort of way but I was dedicated to checking it out. Not every place we stayed was famous for its monastery and I wanted to see the cathedral and receive a pilgrim's blessing from the priest. I'm a spiritual slut; I'll take all forms of prayers and blessings regardless of the setting or dogma.

I put on hiking boots again even as each cell in my body was suddenly in protest and began screaming, "What the hell are you doing? We just sat down and stopped for a while."

It hurt to put those boots on again and each step to the cathedral was painful. Even more so than my traverse down the mountain. I was beyond ready to be done with walking for the day. While on the Camino, I would just get used to the pain and it was often harder to keep going after taking short breaks. I learned not to take a break; it was better to just keep walking. Another metaphor for grief is just to keep it moving even if it hurts.

By this time it was dark, and I didn't know where I was going. I turned towards what looked like the big cathedral and went in that direction. I was correct because I found the wide wooden ornate doors and saw a few people coming out and with it also poured beautiful sounds from a pipe organ. I loved listening to organs especially in Spain on the Camino in very old stone gothic cathedrals. I was relieved and entered the sacred old space. I found a hard wooden uncomfortable pew and sat. I breathed out as I let gravity pull me down onto the cold church bench. I was suddenly even more aware of how tired I was and just how much my feet hurt. I took off my boots and put my feet up and under me. After walking all day my feet wanted to be closer to my head for some reason. They preferred being propped up the wall versus sitting where I was now. I sat cross-legged before God in this place; I felt a bit of shame for a tiny moment as it was probably against some religious rule. But then I checked in and my "God" was proud I'd made it and was happy I was taking care of myself by getting comfortable in this very uncomfortable setting. I even started giving myself a foot massage too.

After feeling a bit more settled, I oriented myself by looking around. The walls were made of dark thick stone bricks and the color of the stained-glass windows was subdued because the light of the day had faded by now. I then began to realize this wasn't a mass. I'd missed it entirely. The priest wasn't at the front even though people were sitting in the pews and the organ was playing liturgical music. There were groups of people coming down the aisles with a tour guide. I felt very disappointed I had walked all that way in hopes to have this blessing only to miss it.

I began to just drop into my life, and I started to cry as I thought about Michael. All day long I walked with the mantra of how to love quadriplegia and how we were going to do this life. I never really came to some kind of conclusion or answer with just how to love quadriplegia. I don't believe it's actually possible to love it, it simply makes sense to learn to live with it each step of the way, just like I was walking each painful step on this Camino.

And surprisingly, I was getting used to the pain. I still felt it but somehow it felt easier, was I just accustomed to it, or was my body hardening to the path somehow? I thought about how as humans we can put up with a lot more than we think we can. I was coming to realize I was much stronger than I thought myself to be.

And then I just felt my love for Michael and the fact that we are both still alive and able to love each other. Our hearts were still the same and having this love was all that mattered. I began to feel the warmth in my heart center the more I thought about him and our relationship.

The warmth in my heart felt like a swarm of sleeping bees waking up slowly – there was an electric humming or buzzing sensation. It's the way you feel after singing for hours at a kirtan. It's a spiritual love. It began in my heart area and then radiated up and down my body as it lit up the entire energetic pathway. It felt like the light at dawn or sunset with pink-tinged fluffy clouds from a Maxfield Parrish painting. It felt peaceful and there was a deep knowing in it; ultimately, I trusted it, us, and this path we were on.

Sitting on the hard church bench inside the cathedral after walking up the mountain and down the leaf-covered path to the cathedral, well, I just gushed open with love, appreciation, and gratitude he's still alive and we still have each other. We still have our hearts, our hearts are still intact. No, actually they weren't, they were even stronger and bigger than before. Now they had more capacity to love and endure. After all, love is a verb, and we are human lovings not just human beings.

Perhaps we were being tested by Spirit. It was asking us, "Will you see love is the key? And your relationship has another plan for you?"

Spirit was pointing us in a very uncomfortable 180-degree turn to do something entirely different with our lives. Our love remained and strengthened us individually, our paths and our relationship, and also our community. Ultimately really nothing else mattered – we have each other, and we found this great love; a soul love. Our relationship was a soul contract. Michael is my soulmate, and I knew I couldn't give him up. Our love was as deep as a wide red rock canyon forged by water and the water was finally nourishing me and my soul. I had finally found what I had been looking for and who knew it would be this – to be in partnership with a quadriplegic man? I wouldn't give this up just because his body no longer worked the way it used to.

And then I felt as if I was in a dream. The music selections being played on the old pipe organ suddenly weren't liturgical at all, they were modern-day pop songs! The organist, who was a young lanky teenager, went from churchy music to singing a song from U2. Then he began playing what sounded like the most beautiful song and was utterly familiar, but I just couldn't remember who sang it originally. The sound of the organ filled up the entire dark space and captivated me as I sat there intently listening and I realized this was the pilgrim's blessing I came for – this spontaneous pop pipe organ concert.

While I sat there listening, massaging my feet, I felt both my tiredness and the buzzing sensation of my love for Michael. I was utterly content as I thought back on the day while I was taking in the epicness of the moment. It was a perfect ending to my day of walking up and down the mountain.

Meanwhile, the teen continued, the music lifting from the old organ. It was beautiful. And I was trying to place the tune, it was very familiar, but I couldn't remember the name of the song. It was the final song he played. And when he stopped, I was very disappointed as I wanted him to keep playing it for at least another twenty minutes. It's as if the entire reason for being in that cathedral was to hear this one song, whatever it was. It brought the soul of the place to life. Otherwise, it was just cold and empty. The song gave a soul to the place, just like our love was holding the temple of our relationship together.

And this simply lodged my love for Michael and our life more deeply into my body, heart, and soul. How do I love quadriplegia? I don't. I never will, but I know we still love each other, and this was enough to figure it out, and simply put, nothing else mattered.

I felt divinely blessed and seen. The Camino had offered its magic message to me, and I received it as deeply as I could. I felt high on this divine intervention as I walked back to sit with my group at the formal dining table in the old hotel adjacent to the monastery. The two who annoyed me the most were already slightly drunk. They had arrived early in the afternoon with their fast-paced walking as if this was some kind of race with the prize of a few bottles of wine. I took my time walking. I honored my own pace and timing. After all, it wasn't a competition, and I wasn't just walking to drink wine even though it was a most welcomed treat at the end of the day. I sat down and joined them on a different kind of high.

I tried to describe my experience to them with words, but it didn't feel right. The moment was hard to translate. And since I couldn't place the song with a group or title, I tried humming it for them. I did so poorly that they all just stared at me bewildered. I was never really good with those humdingers in the brain game called Cranium. I gave up and I settled for sipping my squash soup while keeping my peak experience tucked in as I also tucked my feet under me on my formal dining chair.

I simply drank my red wine and ate more bread. Every evening meal I was full of gratitude for surviving yet another day of pushing my body to walk more miles in one day than I ever thought I could. And today I was filled with even more gratitude for the feat I had accomplished. At our evening meals, we were invited to share any highlights or insights that came through as we walked. Tonight, I shared about the moment in the cathedral and the miracle of my feet, and how they were able to do what they were doing for me.

And even though I was in excruciating pain; I was still grateful for what they were doing for me. My pain was so bad I thought I wouldn't be able to walk the next day. I reached out to Michael and asked him to do some of his remote bodywork on me. He had been starting to work on people without using his body at all. One of our friends at the beginning said eventually Michael would be doing his body work without touching others. This was coming true, and it was truly amazing. I was grateful and relieved the next morning, the pain was gone! And I was able to walk another day.

Now when I find myself struggling, I think about how I walked up and over the mountain that one day long ago in the Basque lands. It's a reminder to me I can handle just about anything. With what I've been through and am going through with Michael, I can handle anything.

I wouldn't know what the actual song was until I had access to the internet later after the trip was over. I kept the tune tucked away in my awareness as I was super curious to know what it was, it felt significant, and I had to know.

CHAPTER 22

MIRACLE ON THE HILL OF FORGIVENESS

"The gold is in the dark."

—Carl Jung

The next day we got an extra early start as we'd be walking twenty-seven miles to the town called Zubiri which felt easy compared to what we did the day before. Today's walk hardly gained any elevation. The journey today seemed leisurely as we walked through many tall birch forests and alongside a river at one point.

We stayed in a hotel in the town center where the layout seemed ultra skinny and scrunched together. I slept horribly because the town's fucking church clock tower would announce itself every hour and then it thought you might forget so it would ring again five minutes later. And it did this all night long! Instead of sleeping, I drafted a letter of complaint to the mayor in my head. It reminded me of the cuckoo clock in my parent's home. If I spent the night there, I would sneak out in the middle of the night to stop the obnoxious sound. I mean, who needs to know what time it is when you're sleeping?

I showed up for breakfast the next morning in a sour mood which turned ever more sour when I noticed it was pouring rain! I didn't want to walk in this weather, and I wished we could have had the day off to just rest, but I also really wanted to get out of this town. Rachael told us to get ready as if she paid no attention to the weather; it was just another day of walking. She did tell us before signing up for the trip we would walk regardless of the weather. We would walk rain or shine. I tried to put myself in a better mood when I thought – well, at least I get to use the rain gear I packed for myself and my backpack. I started walking being cold, tired, and downright miserable.

It helped to know I would be getting a break soon – the plan was to stay two nights in the city of Pamplona, the place where the bulls run in the streets once a year during a festival in July.

We had our much-deserved break – I spent the day off from walking long distances, and instead, I wandered the medieval city center, visited the cathedral and museums, and even received bodywork. I really missed Michael as I had lunch by myself and was doing everything else alone too. I knew he wouldn't have wanted to visit the churches with me.

We had two more full days of walking and then the trip would be over. I felt sad knowing this; part of me wanted to stay and walk to the end of the Earth. And another part of me wanted to get home to see Michael. I started our next day of walking with newfound energy inspired by our one day off and by the thought of finishing this trip. This was also the day I knew I had to drop the rest of the rocks – I had the largest remaining ones in my backpack's pocket.

I started walking with a new fervor. For some reason, I was the one taking the lead today. I didn't take any breaks when the others did because I just wanted to keep going. By this point, I had learned my feet did better if I didn't stop. I also enjoyed knowing the group was behind me. I was inspired to leave small tokens of love for them along the trail

– hearts made of small rocks or pinecones. As I did this, I was thinking about how I wanted to make more art like this when I got home, and I noticed more of my thoughts were turning homeward.

I would learn later Naomi filled my hearts with her rose petals. And the Swiss woman told me, "Your hearts really helped me to keep going."

I loved hearing this — how my creations inspired others to make more art and to just simply keep going with life. I also loved hearing how Naomi and I made art together and I hoped to do more collaborative pieces outside and in nature soon.

The path was a slow and steady incline up to a place called "The Hill of Forgiveness." It was near huge wind turbines and at the top was a beautiful metal sculpture placed there in honor of pilgrims. I planned to get there and then wait for the others to have lunch together.

When I arrived, I intuitively knew this was the place to leave my remaining rocks. This was why I wanted to be the first to arrive; I wanted some time alone with my rock ritual. I found the place that felt right; I took off my pack and sat down. I arranged the rocks along with the ever-faithful Gumby and the Troll Angel and then I knelt to pray. All along the path today I was thinking about forgiveness since we walked towards the hill named after it. I forgave the rock where Michael fell, I forgave earth for gravity which pulled him down and I forgave Michael for biking that day. And then it went beyond my immediate reality, and I found myself forgiving many others and even myself. I was brought back to what Sobonfu taught me in the grief ritual – if you want to forgive others, you must forgive yourself first.

As I placed the last stone on top of the others in a small cairn, I brought up my camera to take a photo to capture the moment. As I took the shot, a mountain biker came into my camera view! I was stunned and gasped out loud as I looked to the skies and said while choking back tears, "Wow! Are you fucking kidding me?! You really see Michael and me don't you? Thank you!"

I just couldn't believe it. I didn't even know you could bike the Camino. I hadn't seen any cyclists until this very moment. I felt seen and heard by Spirit and was beyond grateful for yet another Camino message. I was truly held by this path of stars.

It wasn't long until my group arrived. I shared my moment with a few of them while we arranged our smorgasbord of lunch we'd all carried. It was one of my favorite times of the day—eating yet another meal on the trail in a beautiful place together.

The path down was filled with beautiful rocks and pebbles – they reminded me of the way the earth looked back home. Or was I just homeward-bound at this point? Probably. I was feeling a lot of both/and...I was BOTH looking forward to going home and sharing all of these epic Camino moments with Michael in person AND I was super sad to have to say goodbye to this path. Yet I was beginning to carry the Camino inside of me; the real Camino started when you stepped away from it and entered back into your life.

For the rest of the way down the hill, all I kept seeing along the path were heart-shaped rocks. They jumped out at my vision as if they were mirroring the hidden stars in the sky above. The Camino was telling me nothing else mattered except love.

The next day would be our last walking day and I used it to really contemplate all I had learned and received from this magical trip. Along with knowing I wanted to make more art in sacred natural places, I also began to see my life's calling becoming clearer— I wanted to create rituals and ceremony to help people grieve. My life's path was to not only continue to love Michael but to love others as well. And I was being called to show and teach others how to love deeply, which also meant how to grieve fully.

My Camino ended as we walked towards our final destination — Estella, the town named after the stars. Rainbows led us along the way, and it was as if we walked into a dream. We walked through a few farms where we were escorted by four donkeys, a little girl in a bright green dress who excitedly waved at us, and many iridescent dragonflies. Then we walked near a brewery where large globs of matter were falling slowly from the sky. They looked like handfuls of bathtub bubbles. In my mind they were blessings straight from heaven, little love bombs coming directly from the stars.

Arriving at our final posh hotel that seemed to be a star itself with its shining inviting features inside each room – the gold fixtures in the bathroom and the stark white bed linens holding me like they did in the beginning. My feet were extremely tired, yet my heart was overflowing with gratitude. I was ready to rest and prepare myself for my long journey home the next day. I began to pack my bag for the plane, not the path. My suitcase had expanded as had my feet and my spirit.

The next morning, we said our goodbyes in our final closing circle on the tall steps before the cathedral. It was early and the sun made the stone cathedral walls glow with earthy yellows. This town did indeed shine like a star.

Our goodbyes were rushed as some had to get off to the airport early and the California woman just decided not to come. I wasn't surprised at all, and yet I wasn't disappointed either. All the time spent walking, I was able to work with my projections of others until I was neutral about whatever it was that bothered me. I was able to resolve the issue with the man who just came to drink wine as well. He didn't annoy me anymore either. This was a lesson I would be taking with me —to go for long walks and process my projections of others.

What else was I taking with me? A renewed sense of my life and my expanded love for Michael, a deep appreciation for my able body and all it does for me, and a deepened sense of awe for the natural world and the beauty that held me all along the way. I felt much lighter. I wasn't holding onto the heavy rocks from the trail anymore, yet I was also much lighter in my mind and heart. And I wasn't leaving the Camino, but rather, it was within me now and I'd be taking all I learned back with me. I would keep walking the Camino of my life every day. As one of the Pilgrim's blessings said: Blessed are you pilgrim, because you have discovered that the authentic "Camino" begins when it is completed.

Everything I had learned about the Camino tested me later when I learned Lufthansa Airlines was on strike, and I would be put up in a hotel for the night. I wouldn't be leaving just yet; I was stuck in Bilbao near the airport. And by the time all my arrangements were made, it was late in the afternoon on a Sunday. This meant many places would be closed. Instead of going back to the city to sightsee or take a taxi to the ocean, I chose to do what I'd done ten days previously — I went for a walk. I walked for about 4 hours around the neighborhood near the hotel.

Later, I woke up in the middle of the night with a deep hypnagogic thought. We'd been walking with a phrase Rachael had given to us to think about —the word was 'Guapacha,' which basically means unfuckable. I woke up with an insight – Unfuckable is a choice; I can always choose to stay calm.

Fifteen minutes later I would put this into practice — the fire alarms went off, the loud obnoxious beeping sounds screaming for us to get the fuck out of there as fast as we could. So there we all were, all these tourists in our pajamas sleepily going down the stairs to safety in the parking lot. Turns out someone had simply burnt their food in the kitchen; thankfully we were allowed to go back in quickly. It was about 4:30 a.m. and my alarm was set for 5 a.m. to get to the airport. It was a rude awakening, and I learned another important lesson – always have your important documents and things ready to grab quickly in case you need to jump out of bed to flee the hotel. In my flustered state, I hadn't grabbed anything at all.

After this, all went well. I arrived home safely albeit a day late. Many hours later I had my sweet homecoming and reunion with Michael. I dropped my bags and rushed over to hug him— I straddled him on Mobe, and we sat together with our foreheads pressed together for quite a while. I was full of stories, love, and renewed gratitude for this precious life of ours.

CHAPTER 23

HONORING OUR UNION
AND OUR GRIEF

"Nothing Else Matters."

—Metallica

About a year into our relationship, Michael and I attended a beautiful wedding ceremony for some of his closest friends. It was a spectacular day in October. The fall colors on the trees were vivid with brilliant yellows, reds, and oranges. The sun shone brightly yet there was a chill in the air. Michael was driving us home on the back country roads from Fort Collins to Boulder and as we rounded the sharp curve where the road took some serious turns to go around a creek, he asked me out of the blue, "Do you want to be married someday? Like not to me, not now, but I'm just wondering if this is something you want someday."

I was delighted and pleasantly surprised as we'd only been dating a few months. I felt a warmth in my belly. I paused to think before I spoke, and then said, "Yes, I'd like to be married."

And then I asked him back, "Do you want to be married again?"

I knew his divorce had been really hard on him. He answered quickly, which was rare for him, "Yes, I do. I love being in a partnership, so I really want to be married again. But what I don't want is the pressure to have to surprise you with a proposal. If we ever get to that, I'd like us to come to an agreement together. Are you okay with that?"

I appreciated his idea although the young princess part within me, which I didn't even know I had, felt slightly disappointed. Maybe it was all those Hollywood movies with surprising proposals where the man gets down dramatically on one knee. Well, it didn't surprise me that he asked this. And I simply said, "Yes, I'm okay with it."

In early December 2014, I was driving to my Boulder office to see clients. A love song came on the radio and along with it I felt a sense of knowing in my gut. And suddenly my heart began to hum and I blurted out loud to myself, "I want to marry Michael! I'm going to ask him to marry me!"

I began to laugh and cry at the same time. I felt giddy about the truth of it all. I felt a surge of yellow excitement radiating from my belly and heart. I kept this a secret and started my plan to ask him. I thought about suggesting we get matching tattoos on our ring fingers instead of the traditional rings. And for Michael getting a tattoo would be somewhat easy as he wouldn't feel the pain. One benefit of being a quadriplegic? Although some would argue the healing is in receiving the pain of the tattoo. I know many who get tattoos to honor their grief and feel much better after the adrenaline rush.

I knew Michael wanted to be married again and I also knew he didn't want to wear a ring as we had talked about it earlier. I guess my proposal wasn't a total surprise. He declined my idea of getting tattoos as rings. He didn't want the toxins from the ink in his body and he didn't find it humorous at all about the tattoo being painless for him. Sometimes our dark quadriplegic humor was funny and other times it was not.

I got creative then and made two necklaces for us to wear. I bought two small smooth black river rocks and two silver metal bird wing tokens. I tied these together with a black waxed cord and a locket.

On Christmas Eve of 2014, I did just what he asked me not to do. I completely surprised him—after dinner, I squatted in front of him, so I was at his eye level. I gazed into his eyes for a long moment and then I pulled out the necklaces. I said to him, "Michael, I cannot imagine my life without you. You are my other wing, and we fly better when we're together. Michael Mathieu—will you marry me?"

He immediately burst into tears and sobbed as he said, "Yes."

We embraced each other for a long time. Michael was completely surprised because he thought I'd never want to marry him with the state he was in now. This is why I had to propose to him first. I knew I loved him regardless of quadriplegia and I needed to let him know I chose this life and everything that came with it.

He then said we needed to stay true to the agreement we made long ago in his car; he wanted an opportunity to ask me to marry him. Yet we also started planning the wedding. Looking ahead at the dates we couldn't decide what year to do it —2015 or 2016. I'd never planned a wedding before, I didn't know how much time we actually needed. It became crystal clear when I noticed in 2016, August 27th, the date of the accident, would fall on a Saturday. Perfect! We would reframe the day, otherwise known as the dreaded fucking day (DFD for short) as the declaration of our love day (DLD).

The following year my parents were having Christmas Eve dinner with us, we had the traditional Swedish meatballs and rice pudding they always insisted on having. I was wearing my apron with the sculpture of Michelangelo's David in the full monty as I started cleaning up the kitchen. While I was distracted by dirty dishes, he had my mom attach my ring to his stylus or as one of our caregivers calls it – 'his finger'. I had hired a jeweler to make a silver ring with a white river rock the size of a dime, next to a green peridot gem, August's birthstone. This would represent both my birthday and the date of the accident.

He called me over in a more dramatic way than usual and lovingly said, "Get on your knees woman!"

He brought my ring towards me and said, "Would you do me the honor of becoming my wife?"

And, of course, I said yes as my parents rushed over to hug us both. We were a crying heap of love as we all huddled together around Michael.

I have to explain something here – this would not be our "wedding" day. You see, Michael and I cannot officially be married because he would lose his Medicaid benefits. If we were to be married, it would also mean all my assets for the rest of my life would go to the government. So instead, we had a commitment ceremony. I add this here because I want more people to know there are ridiculous laws in place in terms of disability, benefits, and marriage. I rejoiced the day my gay friends could be married in this country, but we still cannot.

Since our "wedding" was very untraditional, I decided instead of the rehearsal dinner party before the ceremony, we would do something entirely radical--we would have a grief ceremony for us and our community. We invited everyone who was invited to the wedding to come witness and honor the grief that affected not just Michael, me, and our families, but all of them as well.

Not everyone wanted to do this. Some people declined due to their busy lives or simply because they didn't want to deal with their grief. Seventy people did come, and I led them in a simple grief ritual. We gathered in a large circle with a small round table in the center. In the middle of the table was a large glass vase of water placed inside another shallow wide bowl. These were both surrounded by small rocks I gathered on the land near us for this occasion.

I walked around the center and said, "This accident didn't just happen to Michael and me, it happened to all of you too. And I want to give you all a chance to say anything you may need to say with us witnessing you. When big grief happens like this, my mentor Sobonfu Somé told me how important it is for Michael to be welcomed back. He…we have been through immense change, and we need you, our community to welcome us back from this initiation."

The next two hours many people took the invitation to speak and be heard. As they came to the center of the large circle, they were invited to grab a rock from the table. As they spoke, they held on to the rock and after speaking they placed it in the large vase full of water. Eventually, the vase was full of stones, and the water overflowed, representing the flow of our grief and tears.

The most vivid statement in my memory was when our friend Christian Glover came up and stood right in front of Michael and with emotion said loudly, "Michael, a terrible fucking thing happened to you."

And then he immediately pivoted to me and said, "Beth, a terrible fucking thing happened to you."

It was very healing to receive the utter truth of his words. It was the statement many were afraid to name. He named the elephant in the room, and we could all breathe a bit better afterward. Many people spoke after this moment and their grief was witnessed.

We ended the evening with the entire group surrounding us; everyone was touching someone who was touching us. And then one of our friends and former caregivers, Karambir, blessed us with a gong bath as he circled us while he played. It was the best 'rehearsal dinner' and I felt ready to focus on our love and commitment after honoring the grief of our community.

The next day at the commitment ceremony, one of my friends, who didn't attend the night before, was speaking to someone who didn't know all the details of Michael's accident and she started to speak about it. I casually walked away from them because I was crystal clear this was what Friday's grief ceremony was for and today needed to celebrate our love. This was the one day I didn't want to dwell on the trauma and the grief. And in the invitation to the events, I was clear about this. Yet, of course, we spoke about it in the actual ceremony. I was very aware I didn't want it to be the focus of this day and I felt proud for simply walking away.

The commitment ceremony took place in the late afternoon in a park near our home where we were witnessed by our families, friends, and community. It was a beautiful late August summer day with a few clouds in the sky. I wore a simple sheer flowing white tunic with cropped white pants and hot pink and black John Fluevog clogs. My hair was pulled up with flowers. I held onto a bouquet made from a deer's antler, ribbons, and wildflowers. Michael also wore white trousers and a light turquoise blue, collar shirt which really brought out the beauty of his eyes. He also wore a straw fedora hat. He looked very handsome.

I felt full of gratitude and happiness as I walked into the ceremony with my parents on either side of me. Tears filled my eyes as I began to hear our song which was chosen for us from one memorable moment in time. Our musician friends played and sang the unique love ballad by the heavy metal band Metallica—*Nothing Else Matters*.

Insert mic drop sound here—Right?! This is the song I heard during the unforgettable moment in the cathedral after climbing the mountain all day. This would forever be our song to remind us that truly nothing else matters because we still have each other.

The ceremony ended with Michael Hahn, my Michael's best man, wrapping us with a long rope of ribbon pieces – the pieces inspired by the ones I left along the Camino. As each guest arrived, they were invited to pick a piece of multi-colored ribbon and infuse it with a prayer for our union. These were tied together into one long rope. I then straddled Michael to sit on him and his chair, which is why I now prefer pants over skirts – it's much easier to sit on him this way. Together we were wrapped in our community's love. We rolled away into the setting sun to have a moment to ourselves with the sign on the back of his chair which said, "Just Committed."

Hours later our beautiful gathering ended with the DJ playing Metallica's love ballad – the sun had set, and the stars were shining in the night sky. All our friends gathered around us, swaying and boldly singing this song to us. It was a beautiful way to end this most amazing day. If I could, I would go back and relive it. It was such a joy to have all our family, friends, and community with us to witness, support and love us. And for us, it meant more because of everything we'd been through, and it was a way to begin to give back to those who really showed up for us throughout this entire process.

A year later, I led my first grief-walking Camino trip with Rachael, and then I would lead another one in 2018. Since it went so well for me on my first Camino trip, I wanted to provide grief-walking pilgrimages for others. And each time I attended the mass, I'd wait to see if the young man would come and play the pipe organ and sing the Metallica song. I wondered at one point – does he do this every day for the pilgrims? And each time I was disappointed by the stark silence after the mass was over, he never came and played those pop songs like that one blessed day. There was nothing like receiving the blessing from Metallica's ballad on the pipe organ filling those old stone-cold walls, even getting into the tiny cracks, and the cracks in my heart. The song blew me wide open to the love and pain of our reality. It filled the entire cathedral and was much better than any official priest's blessing on my head.

One of my favorite places on the Camino where I felt most at home was a restored Basque castle in Spain called Hotel Akerreta. It was abandoned long ago and then it was discovered and restored with devotion to give pleasure and respite to its guests. Being there, I felt comforted by the fireplace, the warmth of the owner, José Marí, and the overall ambiance of the place. It's a much-welcomed gem, especially after walking all day long. It comes with the most delicious beef stew which was slow-cooked all day. I felt like I'd arrived home because I was held by the warmth, comfort, food, and beauty even if it was only for one night.

The way the castle was built is a metaphor for what it's like to have your life blown apart by sudden loss. They intentionally rebuilt it with what remained or what was left behind; they built a treasure out of the rubble by intentionally leaving the cracks in the walls and artfully including them in the decor. You can see the old integrated artistically with the new. It's like grief—you build on what remains after your life goes upside down and all the contents are emptied and tumble to the ground. This process took years to complete, becoming one of the most beautiful hotels.

Just like the hotel, it took us years to adjust to our new life. It took four years to rebuild the castle, and it took us about the same amount of time to rebuild our lives. In the beginning, a nurse at Longmont United Hospital said it would only take a year. She was utterly wrong. It actually took a few years, and we still have moments of adjusting to it even after ten years. It's like a new home and as it settles, it begins to have cracks. Nothing is new forever.

However, one thing remains – our love for each other. Our love continued to grow and became even stronger with each upheaval, each new challenge. We held fast to each other; we held on like the white feather which lives forever amongst the beech trees on the Pyrenees Mountain pass.

Early on, my mom was speaking intently to me, after all, she was worried about her daughter having a really difficult life for the rest of her life. She said to me, "Won't you miss all those activities you used to do together, like dancing, hiking, and traveling? Are you sure you want to do this?"

Without hesitation, I firmly replied, "Our hearts are still the same, and that's all that matters."

HEART VOWS

"Ring the bells that still can ring. There's a crack in everything.
That's where the light gets in."

—Leonard Cohen

Recently I was walking the trail in the foothills near our home in Boulder. I especially love walking this trail in the late afternoon when the sun dips early behind the mountain casting the rest of the land in shadows. The light seems more brilliant then as it squeezes through the trees on the rocky horizon. I walk this trail often for insight and comfort; it has become my constant companion and I try to visit it daily.

This trail is full of grasses, wildflowers in the spring and summer, and Ponderosa pine trees towards the top of the ridge. There is a small creek near it as well; it runs in the spring from mountain snow melt or if we are blessed with an abundance of rain. I love the sound of the flowing waters that whisper to me—keep your grief flowing.

This land for me is also my place of respite from the hub of Michael's needs and our constant revolving door of caregivers. Although by now I am full of gratitude for them, I need a break at times. Without them I would have a very different life; their presence gives me more time to devote to myself, my work, and my spiritual practices. And I would come to learn instead of having our own children, we would have caregivers. Most of them would be pre-med students who we would help launch into adulthood. We became close with so many and are still friends with them today.

About four or five years ago I created another labyrinth on this trail—a simple spiral this time. I made it in an area that was also full of sudden loss and trauma as it was in the destructive path of the 2013 flood. I have watched the plants and trees grow and come back to life just like our life did. Thus, I have a special bond with this place now and it's where I do my best thinking, dreaming, praying, and remembering.

While writing this final part of the book, I was reminiscing about all Michael and I have been through and our current challenges as there always seems to be something. We live with grief every day and we do our best to roll with it.

Recently I remembered Michael's vows to me. I found them in a saved document on my computer complete with the typos from using Siri as his virtual assistant. She never quite gets his voice dictation right and we often laugh because of it. Sometimes she spells my name as 'That' or 'Death,' which I don't mind at all.

But his message was clear, this is what he said, "Beth Erlander. You are my true companion. You're my best friend. You're a weirdo and an absolute goofball! You make me laugh. I love how you delight in yourself at times, talking out loud to yourself, or the plants, finding the voices for people's pets, cracking up to TV shows and movies, and allowing your creativity to shine.

You have stood beside me as my life turned upside down on that fateful day four years ago. Without hesitation, you let me know you have my back and would not leave me. Even when I gave you permission multiple times to move on, you told me to shut up because you weren't leaving.

I'm so proud to walk this journey together with you. You keep rising to the occasion as you open yourself up to the fullness of who you are. It's such a joy for me to be a witness as your friend and lover. You are my true companion.

There were times when I nearly pulled out from this relationship, I had all these reasons, but Spirit made it clear it was not an option as it loudly said, "Michael, you may not leave!"

I am honored and blessed to commit myself to you and our love! We are soul teachers for each other, there is no doubt about it. Whether we only have a few more days or a few more years or many years I choose you! I choose you, warrior woman, goddess of grieving, shining heart, and laughing hyena! I choose you, my true companion!"

And now you're probably wondering where my vows are, yes? Me too. While writing this, I've discovered I've lost them. And just knowing this gives me more grief. It's a reminder of how chaotic life gets when dealing with an overabundance of grief. At the time of our ceremony, I was still grieving and trying to hold space for a full practice where I was helping others amid deep grief and trauma.

Thus, I'm not surprised I misplaced them. I had written them down on a precious piece of paper. I tore apart my basement space searching for them. And then I went through all the files on my computer and even my old hard drive. I then searched for the recording I thought we had of our precious ceremony. That too is lost.

But what I've come to realize is this —it doesn't matter that I lost the paper of my handwritten vows. My words of commitment and love for Michael live permanently inside the roots of my being; deep in my heart where they have grown over these past ten and a half years. And they are intrinsically connected to his. They are written into the base of our being like the roots of the forest trees as they interconnect and support each other in the dark soil beneath them.

We are indeed each other's true companions; soul teachers on this path of life. We have become for each other what Spirit said to me long ago after the weekend getaway where we had our first kiss. The voice came in strong as I said – I want to help Michael be the best Michael he can be, which also meant he was helping me to become the best version I could be.

What I do remember matters and is still true to this day. I will paraphrase them straight from my heart, "Michael you are the most passionate and perseverant person I know. I love you for your tenacity to heal yourself and others. I love your curiosity and your passion for sharing your process and knowledge with everyone you meet. And I love you because you kick my ass, not literally, although I pray someday you will. That would mean your legs would work again...What I mean is you support me in being the best human being possible, you show me the hard truth at times. In doing this, you have helped me to become a better human, and I'm so grateful to you for this. You have shown me what it truly means to love. I say yes to being your partner, your unofficial wife, and in doing so I fully choose ALL of you. I choose this life."

And I still choose this life as we continue to grow in love together.

Michael is now blossoming into a magical healer where he works with the body and its energetic pathways both in person and remotely. He has fully stepped into his healing and is doing his grief work with a shamanic practitioner, Deanna Jenné for about two years. Eventually, we would both work with Deanna as a couple.

Recently, Michael and I have answered the call to work together, offering intuitive and energetic healing sessions. We create a safe container combining our skill set of energetic, physical, mental, emotional, ancestral, and spiritual healing. We're excited to present our work to the world as it unfolds. It comes naturally to us because of our interconnectedness; our energies weave together to hold a space for the person's highest healing potential. Yet it was *Crow* who started it all, which is a long, beautiful story for another time.

I continue to work with those who are deep in grief and I'm in the process of integrating the shamanic healing arts into my psychotherapy practice. The woman dressed in black leather pants with ash on her face from the fire has evolved into a woman dressed in the many shades of white. A small purple pouch hangs from her neck and lays near her heart; it is full of stones and bones and other precious bits. Her hair has grown long and is grey now, it's often piled high on her head like a bird's nest or woven into braids. She has walked through the grief and as she did this the trauma began to fall off her like heavy rocks. She proudly looked in the mirror and saw all the ash on her face. She honored it and then ceremoniously washed it off. She remembers the stones in Mexico with her grief scrawled in charcoal. Both she and the stones have been wiped clean by healing waters. Yet, she still knows the crack exists from the fall that started it all, she holds it reverently because that is truly where the light gets in.

Resources on Grief, Trauma, Quadriplegia, Healing and Shamanism

Books:

Berceli, David—*The Revolutionary Trauma Release Process: Transcend Your Toughest Times*

Cacciatore, Joanne— *Bearing the Unbearable: Love, Loss and the Heartbreaking Path of Grief*

Clark, Cara Hope—*Widow's Moon: a Memoir of Healing, Hope & Self-Discovery Through Grief & Loss; The Transformational Nature of Grief: A Pocket Guide Embracing the Light of Your Soul.*

Choquette, Sonia—*Walking Home: A Pilgrimage From Humbled to Healed*

Devine, Megan—*It's OK That You're Not OK: Meeting Grief in a Culture That Doesn't Understand*

Goodheart, Annette—*Laughter Therapy: How to Laugh About Everything in Your Life That Isn't Really Funny*

Helbert, Karla—*The Chakras in Grief and Trauma: A Tantric Guide to Energetic Wholeness*

Ingerman, Sandra & Wessleman, Hank—*Awakening to the Spirit World: The Shamanic Path of Direct Revelation*

Pajevic, Tanja—*The Secret Life of Grief: A Memoir*

Prechtel, Martín—*The Smell of Rain on Dust: Grief and Praise*

Rysdyk, Evelyn C.—*The Norse Shaman: Ancient Spiritual Practices of the Northern Tradition*

Schildkret, Day—*Hello, Goodbye: 75 Rituals for Times of Loss, Celebration, and Change; Morning Altars: A Seven Step Practice to Nourish Your Spirit through Nature, Art, and Ritual*

Somé, Malidoma Patrice—*Of Water and Spirit: Ritual, Magic, and Initiation in the Life of an African Shaman; Ritual: Power, Healing and Community; The Healing Wisdom of Africa*

Somé, Sobonfu E.—*Falling Out of Grace: Meditations on Loss, Healing and Wisdom; The Spirit of Intimacy: Ancient African Teaching in the Ways of Relationships; Welcoming Spirit Home: Ancient African Teachings to Celebrate Children and Community*

Weller, Francis—*The Wild Edge of Sorrow: Rituals of Renewal and the Sacred Work of Grief*

Practitioners:

Alan Wolfelt, PhD, C.T.
International Author, Educator and Grief Counselor.
Director of the Center for Loss and Life Transition
He has written numerous books on loss and grief.
https://www.centerforloss.com/

Annie Brook Ph.D, LPC, RSME (ISMETA)
Body-Mind Centering teacher, therapist in high regard in the Somatic community.
www.anniebrook.com

Arielle Schwartz, PhD
Clinical Psychologist, EMDR Practitioner, Yoga Instructor
https://drarielleschwartz.com/

Cath Duncan
Artist and Author, Co-founder of the Creative Grief Studio
https://www.cathduncan.com/untangle-your-grief/

Deanne Jenné
Traditional Healer
Initiated shaman in the Huichol tradition and a weather worker in the
Nahua tradition.
https://www.deanna-jenne.com/

Hillary Hurst
Therapist, Metaphysical Healer, Intuitive, and Ritualist
http://hillary-hurst.com/

Kara Chipoletti Jones
Creative Grief Educator, Artist, Author and Co-Creator of the Creative
Grief Studio
https://griefandcreativity.com/
https://creativegriefstudio.com/

Merryl Rothaus, LPC, LMHC, ATR-BC, CHT, ACS
Somatic Art Therapist and Integrative Shamanic Arts Healer
https://www.merrylrothaus.com/

Michael Mathieu
Health Coach and Bodyworker
https://www.michaelmathieu.com/

Rachael Corrine Sanborn
Walking Retreats on the Camino
www.redmonkeywalkingtravel.com

Tanja Pajevic
Writer and Memoir Book Coach
https://tanjapajevic.com/

Victor Warring
Sex and Relationship Coach (Erotic Liberationist)
https://www.rewilderos.com/

Websites:

Craig Hospital
Specialized Hospital for Traumatic Brain Injury and Spinal Cord Injury
https://craighospital.org/

Wags of SCI
Wives and Girlfriends of Spinal Cord Injury
https://wagsofsci.com/

E-Book about Sexuality for those with Spinal Cord Injury
https://sci-bc.ca/resource/pleasureable-sexual-device-manual-for-pwd/

Eye Movement Desensitization and Reprocessing (EMDR)
https://maibergerinstitute.com/

Ecstatic dance
https://ecstaticdance.org/

Rhythm Sanctuary
Dance Community in Denver, Colorado
https://www.rhythmsanctuary.com/

Contact Improvisation Dance
https://contactquarterly.com/

TO MY READERS,

If you are thinking about writing your own grief story…please do so. The world needs more stories of hope and inspiration right now. May this book inspire you to tell your own story in order to heal. May your story become a beacon of light for those who are in the dark depths of grief.

If my story has touched you deeply, please tell others to read it who you believe could benefit from its message. Also please go to _amazon.com_ or _goodreads.com_ and leave your words of praise. All of this will help me as the author. And ultimately I wish that those who need this story the most will find my story to encourage them to keep going.

And if you are stuck in the bowels of grief, reach out to me, there are numerous ways of working with me. Please contact me at beth@betherlander.com.

Many blessings to you all.

Beth

ABOUT THE AUTHOR

Beth Erlander

Beth Erlander is deeply passionate about normalizing grief and helping others to simply befriend it. When we do this, we have access to more life energy and joy-which is our birthright! She believes grief is soul work which is slow work. Ultimately grief is deep medicine.

Professionally, she has a master's degree in Transpersonal Counseling Psychology with a concentration in Art Therapy from Naropa University. She's a therapist, creative grief support practitioner, writer, artist, ritualist, and caregiver.

Although working as a therapist since 1999, Beth believes her greatest training came when her partner Michael crashed his mountain bike, resulting in him becoming quadriplegic. Pulled into this apprenticeship to grief, she found out-of-the-box tools to help her. She found the Dagara Grief ritual from West Africa and walked part of the Camino de Santiago in France and Spain. She began a deeper dive into the elements of nature as a healing guide. She now calls herself a "Grief Creatrix," using ritual, connection to the natural world, the creative arts, and traditional tools like talk therapy, somatic work, and eye movement desensitization reprocessing (EMDR), to help her clients.

During the pandemic, she created an online support group for therapists and wellness practitioners called "Tending the Tenders." It's a grief support group that teaches how to hold grief better for themselves and their clients. She continues to offer this group because she believes the world needs to learn how to grieve now more than ever. We need to hold the many layers of grief – personal, ancestral, generational, and collective.

Beth firmly believes that we cannot do grief alone, and so she strives to create more grief groups, rituals and she also holds grief ceremonies for her community. She co-leads the West African Dagara Grief Ritual taught by her teachers-Sobonfu Somé and Elder Malidoma Patrice Somé, now blessed memories. She is forever grateful to them for all their teachings. Beth was fortunate to study traditional Cowry Shell Divination with Elder Malidoma before he passed and now offers Cowry Shell Divination readings.

Currently, her work is returning to her transpersonal roots she studied in graduate school, placing Spirit in the center. She values the natural world and calls herself an animist-everything is alive. She has relationships with the trees, trails, rocks, waters, mountains, and all creatures near her. She honors her Swedish and German from Russia ancestors. She's learning more from them so she can better understand her grief to help others with their ancestral grief. She values her relationship to Spirit and strives to bring the spiritual into her daily life and work with her clients. She is grateful for the Shamanic path and all her teachers. She is working with a few shamanic practitioners to expand her skills and experience.

She and Michael are currently working together to offer intuitive and energetic healing sessions where they combine their skills of energetic, physical, mental, emotional, ancestral, and spiritual work. Please check out Michael's work about osteopathic bodywork and health coaching here: www.MichaelMathieu.com. And stay tuned for their joint sessions and offerings in the near future.

When she's not tending to her clients or writing she can often be seen walking the trail near her home, hugging the trees, making art with nature, or sitting on the front porch with Michael, their black cat Slinky who adopted them, surrounded by her collection of bones, rocks, and sticks and her many plants in their wild garden.

Moab, Utah 2010   Brainard Lake, Colorado 2023

Beth and Michael before and after the accident.

Made in the USA
Coppell, TX
29 September 2023

22193719R00144